The Grammar Activity Book

Bob Obee

CAMBRIDGE UNIVERSITY PRESS

Cambridge, New York, Melbourne, Madrid, Cape Town, Singapore, São Paulo

Cambridge University Press
The Edinburgh Building, Cambridge CB2 8RU, UK

www.cambridge.org
Information on this title: www.cambridge.org/9780521575799

First published 1999
10th printing 2007

Printed in the United Kingdom at the University Press, Cambridge

A catalogue record for this publication is available from the British Library

ISBN 978-0-521-57579-9 Resource Book

Thanks and acknowledgements

I would like to thank Nóirín Burke, Tina Ottman and Isabella Wigan from Cambridge University Press for all their hard work in the editing and production of this book. A special thanks to my wife Annette and my daughter Lauren for all the hours spent encouraging, playing and sticking, and to my many students in France, Malaysia and Greece who were at the cutting edge of this book's design.

Bob Obee, September 1998

The author and publishers are grateful to all the teachers, students and institutions from all over the world who reviewed and pilot tested material from *The Grammar Activity Book*. Many of the useful suggestions have been taken up and worked into the activities. We would like to thank:

Mark Appleby, Castelldefels, Spain; Steve Barratt, Embassy School of English, St. Leonard on Sea, UK; Raquel Carlos de Oliveira, Sociedade Brasileira de Cultura Inglesa, Rio de Janeiro, Brazil; Eton F Churchill, Kyoto, Japan; Leyla Engin Arik, Istanbul, Turkey; Alan Hart, The British Council Language Centre, Kuala Lumpur, Malaysia; Rosemary Hurst, Wigan, UK; Grażyna Kanska, Warsaw, Poland; Mike Kirby, The British Council, Oporto, Portugal; Ilona Kubrakiewiez, Warsaw, Poland; Jon Leachtenauer, Miyagi-ken, Japan; Andrew Littlejohn, Pisa, Italy; Paula Martín Rosado, Salamanca, Spain; Caroline Nixon, Star English, Murcia, Spain; Santiago Remacha Esteras, IES Pilar Lorengar, Zaragoza, Spain; Sandra Wagner, International School of London, UK; Nibea Yermos and Leonor Corradi, Buenos Aires, Argentina.

The author and publishers are grateful to the authors, publishers and others who have given permission to reproduce texts and other copyright artwork. While every endeavour has been made, in the case of any omission the publishers would like to express their apologies and would welcome information from copyright sources. Our acknowledgements are as follows:

For activity 1.2 (Wildlife whoppers, p. 10) and 10.3 (Royal behaviour, p. 82), extracts from *The Guinness Book of Oddities* © 1995 Geoff Tibballs and Guinness Publishing Ltd; for activity 7.2 (Record breakers, p. 52), records from *The Guinness Book of Records* 1990 edition © 1989 Guinness Publishing Ltd. *The Guinness Book of Records* is a Trade Mark of Guinness Publishing Ltd. Also for activity 7.2 (Record breakers, p. 52), and activity 14.1 (Beyond belief, p. 112), records from *The Alternative Book of Records* by Mike Barwell, © Ralf Laue, see http://www.imn.htwk-leipzig.de/~saxonia/homepage.html on the Internet for latest record changes; for activity 8.3 (Building captions, p. 66), cartoons taken from *The Giant Book of Cartoons and Jokes* © Peter Haddock Ltd., Bridlington, England.

Illustrations:
Doreen McGuiness: page 11.
Phil Healey: pages 18, 19, 37, 38, 39, 54, 55, 59, 64, 71, 77, 79, 83, 87, 97, 102, 103.
Jamie Sneddon: Pages 12, 13, 15, 16, 40, 41, 42, 43, 48, 50, 52, 53, 69, 85, 90, 91, 93, 101, 104, 105, 108, 109, 124, 125.

Cover illustration:
Virginia Tasker.

Concept page design: Amanda Hancock
Produced by Gecko Limited, Bicester, Oxon

The Grammar Activity Book

Map of the book

KEY : E=ELEMENTARY; P=PRE-INTERMEDIATE; I=INTERMEDIATE; U=UPPER-INTERMEDIATE

Introduction

Why use this book?

There are many obvious reasons for introducing gaming as a staple activity in the language learning classroom, particularly with young learners. Games can provide purposeful contexts in which to use language; they stimulate interaction; they promote variety of attentional focus in classroom activity; they engender enthusiasm and they are fun. Games allow learners' personalities to come into play in the course of language-learning activity and, by confronting them with meaningful choices to make through language, engage what they know of the world. It is hoped that the games in this collection will bring all the above in some measure to your teaching context.

Who is this book for?

This book is for teachers of English whose learners are in the 12–16 age range. This is not to say that teachers will not find many of the activities useful with other age groups, but the book has been written primarily with the 12–16 age group in mind. It is hoped, moreover, that teachers of all groups of learners in this age range will find much of use in this wide-ranging selection of activities. The activities in this collection have been written above all with *flexibility* and *adaptability* in mind with regard to *language level*, *size of class* and *cultural background*.

What level is it aimed at?

The book provides a range of activities for use with learners from elementary to upper-intermediate level. Each of its 15 units is built around a particular language area, with a spread of activities targeting different aspects of that language area. Thus, in Unit 4, **MAKING COMPARISONS**, **Line up accordingly (4.1)** – an activity for pre-intermediate learners – targets comparison of adjectives, whereas **Comparative short straws (4.3)** – an activity for upper-intermediate learners – focuses on degrees of comparison (*much*, *far*, etc.) with adjectives and adverbs. Another key feature of the book is that several games have different versions for different levels, and many other activities include useful tips on adapting their language level for other levels of learners.

When would I use this book?

The simple answer to this question is whenever you wish to animate classroom grammar teaching with enjoyable and thought-provoking activities that engage learners both in exploring aspects of structure and using language meaningfully. A slightly more complex answer, however, takes us to the heart of issues involved in different approaches to grammar teaching and promotes a more flexible view of how and when to integrate such activities into lessons.

When we teach grammar, we are generally involved in one of three types of activity. Firstly, we may wish to encourage learners to notice new language – either its structure or use – and come to some initial conclusions about how it works. Secondly, our purpose might be to provide learners with opportunities to manipulate new forms and integrate this language into the system of language they already know. Thirdly, we might ask learners to bring their grammar, along with their other linguistic resources, to bear on some meaningful task, hoping that in the process of focusing on meaning, they will experience the interplay of all their language competencies in the achievement of some communicative goal.

Classroom games and language games in particular, have traditionally been deployed in the service of this third type of activity, helping learners to proceduralise their grammar knowledge in ongoing communicative situations. The activities in this collection, however, are rich in variety and diverse in type and teachers will, therefore, find some games can be deployed for helping students to *notice* aspects of language (see **8.4: Open 'the' doors**, **5.1: Sort yourselves out**, **5.3: Collocation bridges**, **11.2: Opposite moves**) and others for helping students to manipulate new forms (see **8.3 Building captions**, **3.3: Last week's news**), in addition to the many which simply create frameworks for lively ongoing student interactions. With certain games that have open-ended outcomes, there is no reason why they cannot be played initially with the language produced and problems encountered being looked at and discussed (noticed) and subsequently played again with more of the manipulation purpose in mind (see **7.5: Adverb rummy**, **7.1: Point in a story**, **2.4: Zig-zag questions**). Also, many games have different stages that allow teachers to monitor learners' language in different ways at different times (see **4.2: Psychic partners**, **8.2: Pieces of me**). The games in this collection can, therefore, be integrated in many ways into grammar lessons, in some cases providing an initial focus, and in others a fully integrative communicative framework.

Is it suitable for my learners?

The 'content' focus of this book relates to the interests and general knowledge of younger learners by drawing on popular curricula themes such as wildlife, geography, history and sport and by drawing on universally popular cultural areas such as music, film and certain types of literature. Wherever it cannot be assumed, however, that the content is likely to be familiar to learners of all cultural backgrounds, then part of the activity involves learners and sometimes teachers animating the structure with their own cultural content. For example, **2.3: *Do* card quiz** is an activity based on general knowledge of popular music and film, which initially involves groups of learners writing questions for other groups in the class.

How is the book organised?

The first 14 units in the book focus on a specific language area. Each unit contains four or five activities, with each activity focusing on a different aspect of the language area. The final unit contains activities that can be used to revise language taught throughout a course. The book is organised according to language rather than activity type, because it is usually in terms of the former that teachers experience the need to supplement other work done in class. Also, grouping activities together that focus on different aspects of the same language area should enable you as a teacher to identify more readily activities relevant to the needs of your learners.

The *focus box* at the start of each activity gives information on the level, language focus and class size for the activity, as well as an indication of the areas of pronunciation that the activity is likely to involve. Before the start of an activity, or after it has concluded, teachers may choose either to highlight the pronunciation features of the target language or to look at examples of learners' language that were produced during an activity. With each activity, step-by-step *Before class* and *In class* instructions are given, as well as an indication of how much preparation time and class time the activity should take.

What types of activity do the games involve?

The games involve students in various types of gaming activity: board games, card games, racing games, deduction games, puzzle solving, question games etc. They also utilise various types of classroom procedure: working in pairs, groups, mingling in larger groups, collecting things around the room, finding partners etc. This in turn involves learners in different types of interaction: asking questions, answering questions, negotiating, challenging, accepting, refusing and deciding together. No two activities are the same, but all activities involve learners working with other learners in a gaming framework – more often than not competitive – where language is used in the ongoing context of the game.

What about large classes?

It is not uncommon for teachers of learners in this age range to find themselves teaching very large classes. To cater for this, all activities in this collection work with both smaller and larger groups. Many of the board games in this collection, for example, feature one pair of learners playing against another pair, rather than individual learners as opponents. As well as providing for more channels of communication within the activity framework, this also gives the teacher of larger classes a more manageable number of groups to monitor. Similarly, activities where learners 'mingle' are potentially difficult for teachers of larger classes. Any activities in this collection that require learners to mingle keep other students on the sidelines involved in another aspect of the game, thus avoiding potential difficulties with space and student numbers.

Can I find the time?

The activities presented in this book do **not** fall into the categories of warmers, fillers, ice-breakers or Friday-afternoon diversions. They should be used as an integral part of a lesson or series of lessons focusing on particular language areas. Students may often want to note down language brought out by the activities and as teachers, you may well find you want to display things students produce in the course of the activities, and suggest to students follow-up tasks to do at home. Whether or not you have time to use these games in your own teaching contexts is a matter for you after considering the time the games take to play (see map of book) and their intrinsic merit as sources of purposeful activity and meaningful interaction in class.

How much photocopying will I have to do?

All activities involving photocopying contain material to be photocopied on pages separate from the instruction pages. Photocopying has been kept to a minimum, often involving no more than four or five pages in total for an activity, but where possible teachers might want to think about making copies of reusable material (such as game-boards) on more durable card and things such as picture prompts might be usefully copied onto reusable OHTs. For some activities, alternatives to photocopying are suggested, such as writing words directly on cards or using the whiteboard.

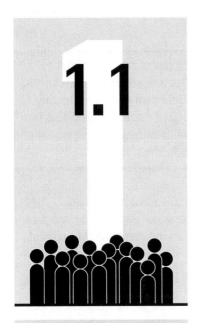

1.1

Global animal bingo

Before class
Make one copy of one **Bingo card** (p.9) for each learner or each pair of learners, depending on the size of the class.

In class
1 Explain to learners that they are going to play a game like bingo, which is popular throughout the English-speaking world. The game here, however, also involves learners asking questions. If bingo, or an equivalent, is played in your country, you can tell learners about it.

2 Give each learner a **Bingo card**. On it there is a grid of phrases. Beneath the grid is a sentence about an animal and three pieces of information about that animal: what it has/has got, eats, likes doing, or where or how long it lives. During the game, each learner will assume the identity of the animal on his/her card.

3 The aim of the game is to be the first learner to cross off all the phrases on his/her **Bingo card** and tell the class which animal each phrase referred to.

4 During the game, each 'animal' must introduce himself/herself. However, it is very important that learners do not reveal any other details about the animal.

On introduction, other learners in the class should pose questions to the animal, based on phrases in their Bingo cards. For example, for the African elephant, the following is written:

*Hello, I'm an African elephant: I have a **small tail**, I eat **leaves** and I've got **relatives in India**.*

The learner introducing himself/herself says: *Hello, I'm an African elephant ...* The other learners then scan their Bingo cards for any phrases that might relate to the African elephant, and ask the elephant any questions that the phrases suggest.

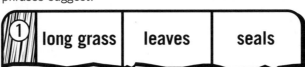

A learner with these bingo squares thus might ask: *Do you eat leaves?* The African elephant answers: *Yes, I do.* (This is a detail on the card.) and all the learners who have this bingo square can cross it off.

Another learner with these same bingo squares might ask: *Do you eat long grass?*

The African elephant answers: *No, I don't* (because this is not a detail in front of him/her).

After a question from three or four different learners, move on to another learner, who introduces himself/herself: *Hello, I'm a polar bear,* and so on.

5 If there is more than one African elephant etc. in the class, this simply means that learners may ask the African elephant questions again.

Level
elementary –
pre-intermediate

Class size
whole class

Language focus
present simple *Have ... got*
questions about facts and
habitual actions

Pronunciation
weak forms: *do you* /dju/
you /jə/

Preparation time
5 minutes

Game time
20 minutes

Bingo cards

BINGO ①

under ice	small tail	grass
sitting down	bamboo	seals
long grass	dancing	queen

*Hello, I'm a pelican: I live in **Romania**, I eat **fish** and I like going on **holiday**.*

BINGO ②

Romania	leaves	relatives in India
holiday	queen	group
zebras	fish	longer than people

*Hello, I'm an African elephant: I have a **small tail**. I eat **leaves** and I've got **relatives in India**.*

BINGO ③

China	holiday	longer than people
Romania	long sleep	seals
leaves	fish	yellow and brown

*Hello, I'm a bee: I have a **queen**, I like **dancing** and I like **flowers**.*

BINGO ④

grass	dancing	under ice
flowers	small birds	long sleep
zebras	leaves	white relatives

*Hello, I'm a giant panda: I live in **China**, I eat **bamboo** and I like **sitting down**.*

BINGO ⑤

long grass	holiday	bamboo
leaves	small tail	group
white relatives	grass	small birds

*Hello, I'm a polar bear: I like swimming **under ice**, I eat **seals** and I like a **long sleep**.*

BINGO ⑥

under ice	China	relatives in India
sitting down	small tail	long sleep
flowers	longer than people	group

*Hello, I'm a rhinoceros: I eat **grass**, I have **white relatives** and I like **small birds** on my back.*

BINGO ⑦

zebras	long grass	under ice
small birds	sitting down	fish
relatives in India	China	queen

*Hello, I'm a tortoise: I live **longer than people**, I have a **yellow and brown** shell and a **long neck**.*

BINGO ⑧

long grass	dancing	Romania
long neck	relatives in India	grass
yellow and brown	small birds	seals

*Hello, I'm a lion: I live in a **group**, I like **long grass** and I eat **zebras**.*

1.2 Wildlife whoppers

Before class
Make one copy of the **Fact cards** (on p.11) for the whole class and separate the cards from the pictures.

In class
1 This game is about separating true facts from false ones. Similar games may be played in your country. If so, point this out to the class at the start of the game.

2 Before the game starts, you might like to look at the key wildlife vocabulary (verbs) that the game will involve. You could ask learners which of the following words could be used to talk about birds:

lay   hatch   migrate   hibernate   feed on   sting   give birth   leap   glide   nest

Divide the class into three or four roughly equal teams and give each team an equal number of game cards with the accompanying pictures. Tell learners that they should discuss their game cards quietly in their teams so that players in other teams cannot hear what they are doing.

3 The aim of the game is to try to get other teams to believe that 'false facts' are true.

4 Explain to learners that each card contains two sentences (facts) about an unusual animal/fish/bird. These two sentences are true and cannot be changed.

The cards also, however, contain various other prompts that learners might use to make up a third fact about the animal on the card which is false (factually untrue). The teacher should go round the different teams helping learners as they write their 'false facts'. Thus, when the game is ready to start, each card has one 'false fact', in addition to the two true facts.

Nominate one team to start. Ask the team to show the picture accompanying its first card to the whole class. Then ask one team member to read the three facts to the rest of the class (he/she will need to do this twice). Stress to the class that facts should be read out in random order. Members of other teams should then consult and agree which fact they believe to be false. When each of the other teams has told the class which fact they think is untrue, the team with the card should reveal which fact was false.

Then ask another team to read out a card, and so on.

5 Keeping score: Teams correctly identifying the false fact score one point. If no team correctly identifies the false fact, the team with the card scores two points. Obviously, the team that writes the subtlest and most genuine-sounding false facts will be the winner.

Level
intermediate – upper-intermediate

Class size
whole class

Language focus
use of present simple to talk about general truths and facts

Pronunciation
third person 's' ending: /s/ /z/ /iz/

Preparation time
5 minutes

Game time
25 minutes

Fact cards

The flying frog (*Rachophorus pardalis*)

Flying frogs lay their eggs in trees.
Flying frogs have sticky toes.

leap   move   have/possess

The armadillo (*Dasypopidae*)

Armadillos are always born in fours.
The armadillo holds its breath underground.

catch   feed on   lives in

The wandering albatross (*Diamedia exulans*)

The wandering albatross sleeps while flying.
It lays eggs which hatch four months later.

glide   live   travel

The bower-bird (*Ptilonorhynchus*)

The bower-bird builds a hut not a nest.
The male bird gives the female flowers.

lay   fly   hide

The quetzal (*Pharomacrus mocino*)

The quetzal has a tail twice as long as its body.
The quetzal jumps backwards out of trees.

lose   keep   nest

The elephant (*Elephans maximus*)

An elephant drinks 90 litres of water a day.
Elephants sometimes dig for water.

bury   give birth   travel

The Mallee fowl (*Leipoa ozellata*)

The Mallee fowl buries its eggs.
The Mallee fowl does not feed its young.

migrate   lay   nest

The mudskipper (*Periophthalmus*)

The mudskipper climbs trees.
The mudskipper catches food on land.

eat   swim   use

The robber crab (*Birgus latro*)

The robber crab climbs trees.
The robber crab eats coconuts.

carry   store   hide

The ribbonworm (*Nemertea*)

The ribbonworm eats itself when hungry.
The ribbonworm shrinks when there is no food.

feed on   live in   protect themselves

The European eel (*Anguilla anguilla*)

The European eel crosses the Atlantic to lay its eggs. It dies after laying its eggs.

swim   float   carry

Rattlesnakes (*Crotalinea*)

Rattlesnakes eat dogs.
Rattlesnakes hibernate in large groups.

sting   catch   sleep

Extracts from *The Guinness Book of Oddities* © 1995 Geoff Tibballs and Guinness Publishing Ltd.

The robber crab

The mudskipper

The rattlesnake

The ribbonworm

The quetzal

The elephant

The armadillo

The flying frog

The wandering albatross

The Mallee fowl

The European eel

The bower-bird

1.3

Adverb backgammon

Level
intermediate –
upper-intermediate

Class size
groups of four

Language focus
use of temporal adverbs
with present simple/
present continuous

Pronunciation
third person ending –
contrast *goes / comes* /z/
with *takes / shouts* /s/

Preparation time
5 minutes

Game time
25 minutes

Before class

Make one copy of the **Game board** (p.13) and one copy of both sets of counters for each group of four students. You will also need to bring one dice for every four learners to class.

In class

1 This game is inspired by the game of backgammon. It is a game where players bring counters on, move them round the board and take them off according to the roll of the dice. Many versions of this game exist throughout the world. If this game exists in your country, refer to the game by its more familiar name.

2 Divide learners into pairs and arrange the class so that one pair is seated around the board, facing another pair against whom they will be playing. One pair moves around the board in one direction, and the other pair in the opposite direction.

3 The aim of the game is to be the first to have brought all your counters on and moved them past the final opposite quarter of the board.

4 This game is much simpler than some versions of the real game you may have played. For example, this game begins with all counters off the board and there is no 'taking' of an opponent's counters in this game. To highlight how simple this version is, draw a rough sketch of the game board on the blackboard and explain the following:

Player A comes on here …   …and moves this way round the board

Player B comes on here …   …and moves this way round the board

Player A finishes when last counter crosses this line

Give each pair a different set of counters.

Pairs take it in turns to roll the dice and move counters around the board. A pair brings a counter on one of the first six bars of their half of the board, according to the roll of the dice (one to six). However, a counter can only be brought on and subsequently moved to another bar if the adverb on the counter grammatically fits the sentence on the bar.

When a pair feels that the opposition has made an ungrammatical move, they should challenge this. If, after discussion and/or adjudication by the teacher, the move is found to be ungrammatical, the challenged pair must move the counter back to where it was and miss their turn. A pair cannot move a counter onto a bar already occupied by an opponent's counter.

Each pair can move or bring on any counter at any time, but it must move one counter the exact number of bars indicated by the roll of the dice. If the pair cannot do this, it simply forgoes a turn.

Game board

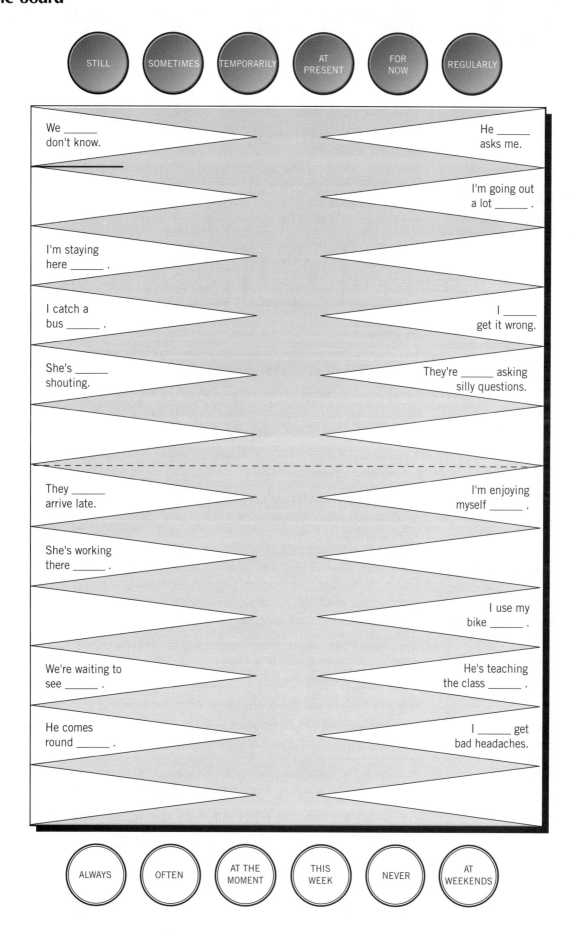

STILL   SOMETIMES   TEMPORARILY   AT PRESENT   FOR NOW   REGULARLY

We _____ don't know.

He _____ asks me.

I'm going out a lot _____ .

I'm staying here _____ .

I catch a bus _____ .

I _____ get it wrong.

She's _____ shouting.

They're _____ asking silly questions.

They _____ arrive late.

I'm enjoying myself _____ .

She's working there _____ .

I use my bike _____ .

We're waiting to see _____ .

He's teaching the class _____ .

He comes round _____ .

I _____ get bad headaches.

ALWAYS   OFTEN   AT THE MOMENT   THIS WEEK   NEVER   AT WEEKENDS

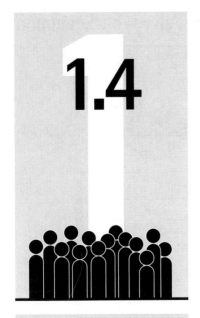

1.4 Behind the screen

Level
elementary

Class size
whole class

Language focus
present continuous
questions (things
happening around now);
present simple questions
(habitual actions)

Pronunciation
is /ɪz/ *does* /dʌz/
going /gəʊ-ɪŋ/

Preparation time
5 minutes

Game time
20 minutes

Before class

Revise the following key vocabulary needed for the game: verbs such as
hold stand sit use wear and temporal adverbs such as **every day once a
week during the day** plus adverbs: **inside/outside**. Then on four separate pieces
of paper or card write the following in large letters:

In class

1 Explain to learners that in this game, they must ask questions to try and
discover a simple activity that someone is doing, based on the categories above.

2 Divide the class into Teams A and B. At the front of the class you need to
make some kind of screen for one learner to sit behind, so that he/she is not
visible to the rest of the class (e.g. by using a portable board).

3 The aim of the game is to find out, by asking questions, what the learner
behind the 'screen' is doing.

4 At the start of each round, ask a player from one team (for example, Team A)
to sit behind the screen and one student from Team B to stand beside the
screen, so that the latter is visible to the rest of the class. The player from
Team B should then hand the player from Team A one of the four cards. The
player from Team A then has to mime a simple action related to the type of
activity on the card, so that the player from Team B understands what he/she
is doing. For example, if the player is handed the 'looking after yourself' card,
he/she might mime 'washing my hair'.

The player from Team B then shows the general activity card to the other
members of Team B and they have to find out what the member of Team A is
doing by asking questions.

Learners initially ask questions about what the person is doing now.
The question must be of the type that requires a *yes/no* answer. For example:

   Is he/she holding something? No, he/she isn't. etc.

As soon as the team gets a *yes* answer, however, members can ask one 'habitual'
question about the action: *Does he/she do it every day?* (Answer *yes* or *no*.)

The game then continues with more 'is doing now' questions. A team can only
ask three habitual questions in each round. After that, team members should
be allowed one more question to guess the action before the round is stopped.

Teams take it in turns to mime.

5 Scoring: if a team guesses the mime with its questions, it scores a point. If
it does not, the other team scores two points.

So what's the question?

Before class

Make one copy of the **Game board** (p.16) and one set of the **Personal question** and **Public place question** cards (p.17) for each group of four learners. Cut the question cards up and keep them in their two separate piles (Personal and Public place). You will also need to bring one dice and sets of counters for each group to play the game.

You may wish to make up some of your own answer/question cards to suit your teaching situation. Care must be taken, however, to come up with answers that relate to a very specific question.

In class

1 Explain to learners that they are going to play a board game. In this game, learners will be given answers and then have to find the questions.

2 Give each group of four learners a **Game board**, one dice and two sets of question cards (**Personal question** and **Public place question** cards). 'Personal' questions are things that friends, family etc. might ask; 'Public place' questions are things that people might ask in shops, in the street etc. Put learners into pairs so that during the game, one pair is playing against the other. Tell learners to put the two sets of question cards face-down next to their board.

3 The object of the game is to move around the board and to get a question right after having successfully landed on the centre circle.

4 How to play: one pair rolls the dice and moves the number of squares indicated. If the pair lands on a question square, the opposition picks up a card from the appropriate pile and reads the card out. They only read the answer, and ask the other pair to guess the original question. For example:

If the answer is: *He's tall with dark hair*, what's the question?

The other pair gives an answer (i.e. constructs the question). The opposition then tells them whether they are right or wrong. If they are right, they can move one square forward/one square back or choose to stay where they are. If they are wrong, they move to the nearest black square.

It is then the turn of the opposing pair to roll the dice.

5 The object of the game is to be the first to land on the central circle and get a question right. However, pairs can only progress along the two central lines that lead to the central circle by having finished on one of the double-lined squares at the end of their previous turn. This is why they have the option of moving forward/back, or staying where they are. Learners' first aim in this activity, therefore, is to get to one of the double-lined squares.

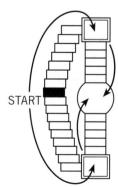

6 When a question has been asked and answered, tell learners to place that card at the bottom of the appropriate pile. If a pair answered incorrectly, they are not told the answer, because the question may come up again.

2.1

Level
pre-intermediate –
intermediate

Class size
groups of four

Language focus
phrasing of everyday and
personal questions and
appropriate answers

Pronunciation
weak forms: *was* /wəz/
were /wər/ linking *do_you*
/dju:/

Preparation time
15 minutes

Game time
30 minutes

15

2.1 So what's the question?

Game board

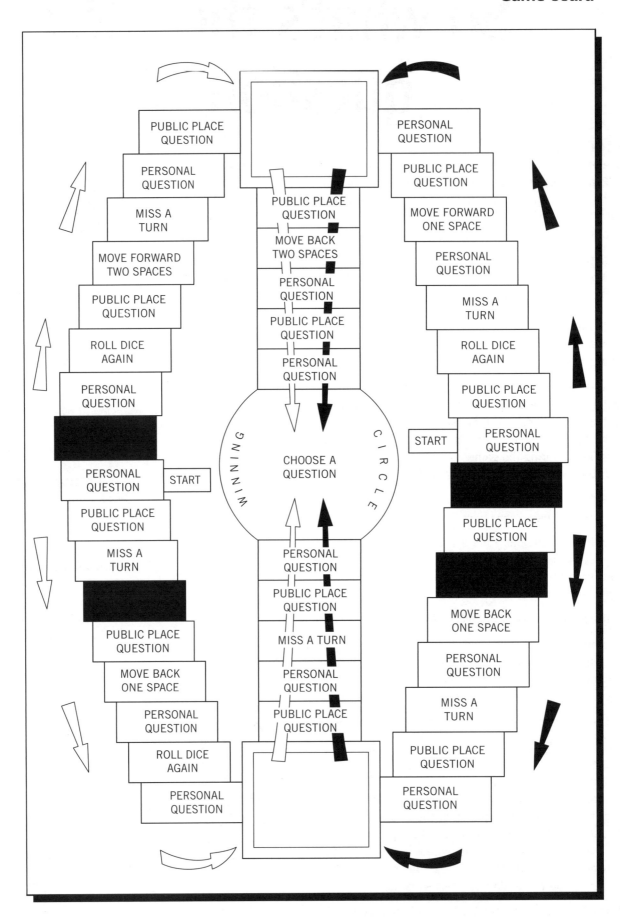

From **The Grammar Activity Book** by Bob Obee © Cambridge University Press 1999

2.1 So what's the question?

Personal questions

Public place questions

---

answer: 6th January.
I'll be 13.
question: When is (it) your birthday?

answer: Usually at six, but I lie in at weekends.
question: What time do you (usually) get up?

answer: No, that's all, thanks.
question: (Would you like) Anything else?

answer: It was the fourth yesterday, so it must be the fifth.
question: What's the date (today)?

---

answer: 55 kilos, but I'm on a diet!
question: What/How much do you weigh?
or What weight are you?
or What's your weight?

answer: 1.55 m but I'm growing.
question: How tall are you?
or What height are you?
or What's your height?

answer: No, not very. About two miles.
question: Is it far/a long way (away)?

answer: No, only notes, I'm afraid.
question: Have you got any (small) change?

---

answer: Yes, at the hairdresser's this morning.
question: Have you had a haircut?
or Have you had your hair cut?

answer: All sorts. Rock, jazz, classical.
question: What kind/sort of music do you like/listen to?

answer: I'm probably a large, this is too small.
question: What size are you?

answer: No, just looking, thanks.
question: Can I help you (with anything)?

---

answer: Not much. I've spent most of it!
question: How much money have you got (left)?

answer: Not till late. I stayed up watching a film.
question: What time/when did you go to bed?

answer: a (for apple), l (for London), t (for Texas).
question: How do you spell it/How is it spelt?

answer: Single, please.
question: (Would you like a) Single or return (ticket)?

---

answer: I was born in Madrid.
question: Where were you born?

answer: Scorpio.
question: Which/what star sign are you?
or What's your star sign?

answer: Plastic, I think.
question: What's it made of?

answer: No, it doesn't. You'll be there in an hour.
question: Does it take long/a long time?

---

answer: £5 – half price in the sale.
question: How much was it/did it cost?
or How much did you pay (for it)?

answer: A bit. My headache has gone.
question: Are you feeling (any) better?

answer: 578–331 ... and there's an answering machine.
question: What's the/your phone number?

answer: No, they're not. Just engaged.
question: Are they married?

---

answer: Good. It only rained one day.
question: What was the weather like?

answer: No thanks, I'm full.
question: Would you like some/any more?
or Would you like anything else?

answer: No, sorry, it's taken.
question: Is this seat free?

answer: No. I eat meat.
question: Are you a vegetarian?

---

answer: Nothing. I'm fine.
question: What's the matter/wrong/up (with you)?

answer: No, it's too tight.
question: Does it fit?

answer: No. Nice to meet you, Jack.
question: Do you know/Have you met Jack?

answer: I came by bus.
question: How did you get here?

---

answer: He's tall with dark hair.
question: What does he look like?
or How would you describe him?

answer: Mine. It was a present.
question: Whose is it?

answer: I'm in 'C' class.
question: Which/what class are you in (at school)?

answer: None. I'm an only child.
question: How many brothers or sisters have you got?

From **The Grammar Activity Book** by Bob Obee © Cambridge University Press 1999 **PHOTOCOPIABLE** 17

2.2

Sporting chances

Level
pre-intermediate

Class size
groups of four

Language focus
present continuous
questions/simple
questions: verb *to be*
short answers:
yes, we are; no, we're not

Pronunciation
weak forms:
you /jə/ *your* /jə/

Preparation time
10 minutes

Game time
25 minutes

Before class

For each pair of learners, make a copy of a set of **Sports equipment cards** and also a **Game board** (both on p.19).

In class

1 This is a game based on well-known sports involving both strategy and chance. Before you start: write on the blackboard the items of sports equipment featured in the **Sports equipment cards**. Check that learners understand the words and can tell you some of the sports in which these items can be used.

2 Put learners into pairs. Explain that they are going to play a game against another pair. Arrange the class so that one pair of learners is facing the other.

Distribute one **Game board** to each pair of learners. Tell learners that the game depends on them concealing their **Game board** from the other pair. Suggest ways of concealing the boards – with a book or bag.

3 Give out the **Sports equipment cards**. Tell learners to place the cards on a sport in which the equipment may be used. Some cards can obviously be placed on more than one sport. For example, 'gloves' can be placed on the 'skiing', 'football' (goalkeeper), 'ice hockey' square etc. But only one item can be placed on any square.

Make it clear to learners that their boards are now 'set' and they cannot move any of their cards once the game starts.

The idea of the game is to capture all the opposition's **Sports equipment cards** before they capture yours. To do this, players have to guess and subsequently work out on which sport their opponents' cards have been placed:

One pair asks a question:	*Are you playing football with your boots?*
Other pair answers:	*No, we're not.*
Other pair now asks a question:	*Are you going skiing with your gloves?*
First pair answers:	*No, we're not.* (etc.)

When one pair finds an item i.e. gets a 'Yes, we are' answer, they capture the card.

As well as capturing the card, however, they also get the chance to ask a bonus question relating to the squares immediately either side of the square on which the object was captured. For example, if the boots were captured on the skiing square in the example on the right, they might ask the question *Is your helmet next to your boots?* If the helmet is on either of the squares, this is also captured.

4 The winners are the first pair to capture all eight **Sports equipment cards**.

Sports equipment cards

Game board

2.3

Do card quiz

Level
pre-intermediate – intermediate

Class size
groups of three or four

Language focus
subject questions about popular film and music culture

Pronunciation
intonation pattern in *wh-* questions: *who played the Joker in Batman?*

Preparation time
10 minutes

Game time
40 minutes

Before class

Make one copy of the **Question prompt sheet** (p.21) for each team of three to four students. Cut out about 15 small squares of paper or card for each group. Make one copy of the set of **Do cards** (also p.21) for the whole class.

Do cards: There is no cultural bias in this activity in terms of popular music and film knowledge, because it is the learners themselves who are providing the questions. You may feel, however, that different *Do* cards might work better with your group. Teachers familiar with this activity have often used *Do* cards to reinforce vocabulary that has previously been seen or taught.

In class

1 Explain to learners that they are going to play a quiz game based on their knowledge of popular music and film.

2 Divide learners into teams of three or four and give each team a **Question prompt sheet** and about 15 small squares of paper or card. Ask learners in their teams to write 10 to 15 questions, each on a separate card/piece of paper, using the question prompts on the prompt sheet. Tell learners they should keep the 'film' questions and the 'music' questions they write in two separate piles.

When all the teams have written their questions, you are ready to begin the game. Ask each team to give themselves a name and write this on the board.

3 The aim of the game is to be the team that can perform the most *Do* actions correctly.

4 Nominate a team to start. Team B for example, chooses which type of question they want (either 'music' or 'film'). Team A then asks them a question on this chosen category. If Team B cannot answer, or answers wrongly, Team C may try to answer (move clockwise around the class).

If a team answers correctly, the members must take a *Do* card from the teacher. The team must perform the action that is on the *Do* card (for example, 'snore'). If the members succeed, they receive one point. Failure to 'do' results in no points.

Continue to move clockwise around the class, with teams posing and answering questions.

5 Keeping score: Under the name of each team, write all the *Do* actions the members are asked to perform. For those actions teams can perform, put a tick; for those they can't do put a cross. In this way, you will build up what can be quite amusing profiles of what teams can and can't 'do'. For example:

Team A
Give someone five ✓
Do an opera impression ✗
Ask someone out ✓

The winners are the team with the most ticks at the end.

Question prompt sheet

Film:	Music:
Which actor ...	Which album ...
Who starred ...	What instrument ...
Which actress ...	Which single ...
Whose voice ...	Who plays ...
Who directed ...	What's the first line ...
Which character ...	Who sings ...
What happens ...	Which singer/group ...
Which film ...	Which classical composer ...
Who played ...	Who had a hit ...
Where/In which city ... (set)	
Who wrote ...	
(music/soundtrack)	

Do cards

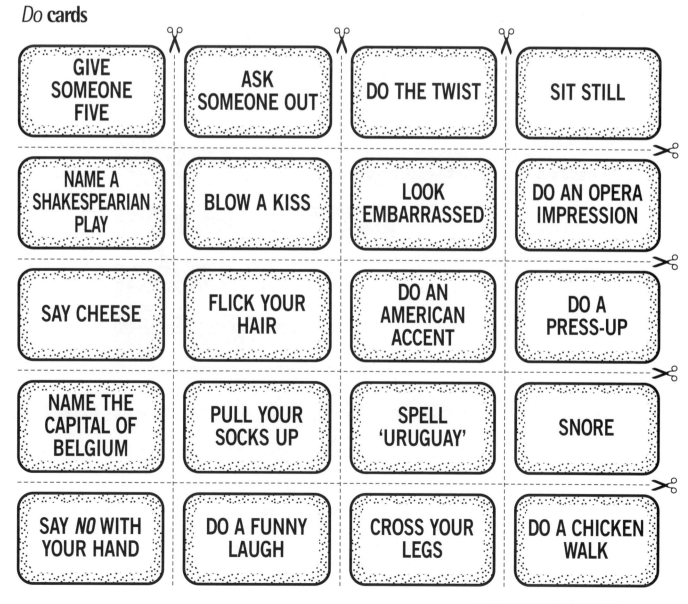

GIVE SOMEONE FIVE	ASK SOMEONE OUT	DO THE TWIST	SIT STILL
NAME A SHAKESPEARIAN PLAY	BLOW A KISS	LOOK EMBARRASSED	DO AN OPERA IMPRESSION
SAY CHEESE	FLICK YOUR HAIR	DO AN AMERICAN ACCENT	DO A PRESS-UP
NAME THE CAPITAL OF BELGIUM	PULL YOUR SOCKS UP	SPELL 'URUGUAY'	SNORE
SAY *NO* WITH YOUR HAND	DO A FUNNY LAUGH	CROSS YOUR LEGS	DO A CHICKEN WALK

2.4 Zig-zag questions

Level
pre-intermediate

Class size
groups of three

Language focus
ways of saying *yes/no* in response to requests, inquiries etc

Pronunciation
falling intonation with acknowledging statements

Preparation time
15 minutes

Game time
25 minutes

Before class
Make one copy of the **Zig-zag cards** and one copy of the **Zig-zag board** (both on p.23) for each group of three learners.

In class
1 This is a board game where learners match questions to appropriate answers.

2 Divide learners into groups of three and give each group a **Zig-zag board**. Give a set of **Zig-zag cards** to each group of learners and ask one learner to divide them equally between the three learners. They should give the cards out face-down. Each learner should then turn their cards over and arrange these cards in front of them.

3 The aim of the game is to be the first player to have put down all your cards, or to be the player with the least cards when the game comes to an end.

4 One player begins by putting a question on the starting point of the **Zig-zag board**. The next player then has to put down an appropriate answer to the question on an adjoining point. The next player then has the option of making one of two moves. For example,

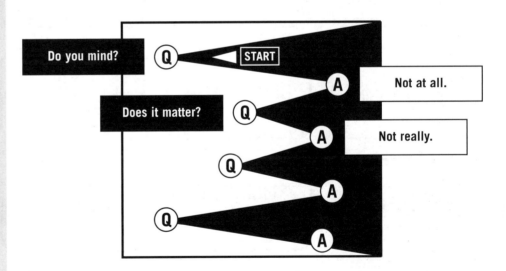

If at any time a player thinks he/she cannot go, the next player simply takes the turn. If a player puts down an unlikely question or answer, the other players may challenge his/her decision. If there is no agreement, the teacher must be called to act as judge. In the case of an incorrect question/answer, the player must pick up his/her card and miss the turn.

5 The winner of the game is the first learner to have put down all his/her question/answer cards. If none of the learners can lay down a card, the player with the fewest cards left is the winner.

The game can be played more than once. Shuffle and redeal the cards each time.

Zig-zag cards

Do you mind?	Not at all.
Shall we?	Why not?
How about you?	I'm afraid I can't.
Would you like to?	I think so.
Is there anything left?	Nothing really.
What would you like?	I'm not sure.
How do you feel?	I'm afraid so.
Do you mean it?	Sure.
May I?	Not a lot.
Does it matter?	Of course.
Can we have a chat?	Not really.
Is that alright?	Yes, actually.
What's the matter?	No problem.
Is there a problem?	I'm fine.
What's it like?	I'd love to.
Is it important?	Great.
What's happening?	Awful.
Are things okay?	Fine.

Zig-zag board

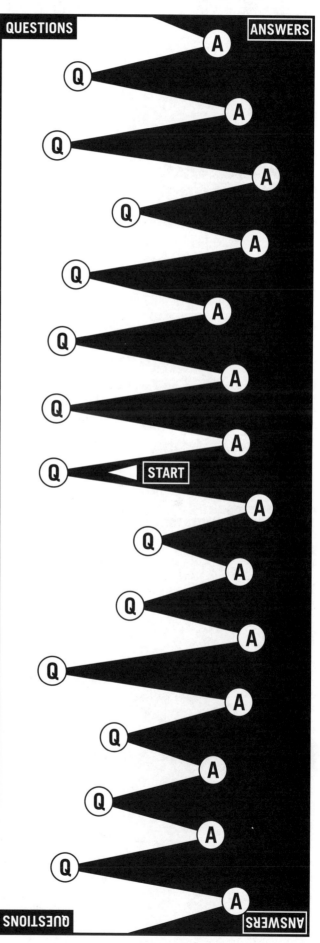

3.1 Round about when

Before class

Make a copy of questions (your own, or the **Example questions** supplied below) to take to class so that you can write them on the board.

Make one or two copies of the **Time phrase cards** (p.25) depending on the size of the class, for the whole class and cut the cards out. Make sure you have some way of pinning or sticking the cards to the black/white board (sticky tape, pins, magnets etc.).

You may wish to introduce other questions for your class but ensure that they fall roughly within the time frame of the game (the last 140 years).

In class

1 This is a general knowledge game where teams have to use their judgment to work out the approximate dates of historical events.

2 Divide the class into three or four teams and give each team an equal number of **Time phrase cards**. Tell them not to show their cards to members of another team.

3 The aim of the game is to be the team that wins the most rounds.

4 Explain that at the start of each round you will ask a question about the date of a historical event, discovery, invention, etc. In their teams, learners have to discuss which of the **Time phrase cards** in front of them roughly corresponds to or is exactly when the event took place.

Each team selects a card and then passes it to the teacher. You then place the cards on the board and reveal when the actual event took place. The winners of the round are learners whose card is the closest in time.

Teams should be encouraged to play a card if they think it is near to the exact date, especially as they have one or two more cards than they need.

5 Teams score one point for each round that they win.

Level
pre-intermediate – intermediate

Class size
whole class

Language focus
adverbial time phrases used with simple past

Pronunciation
linking: *years_ago*; *sixties fifties* /ɪz/

Preparation time
5 minutes

Game time
20 minutes

Example questions

When did the First World War end?	1918
When did human beings first walk on the moon?	1969
When did the first ballpoint pen appear?	1938
When did Alexander Bell invent the telephone?	1876
When did the Berlin Wall go up?	1960
When did the first talking cartoon film come out?	1928
When did Thomas Edison invent the electric lamp?	1879
When were the first TV programmes broadcast?	1936
When did Marconi invent the radio?	1895
When did frozen food first appear?	1924

Time phrase cards

IN THE EARLY '60S	AT THE TURN OF THE CENTURY	IN THE LATE '60S
IN THE LATE '30S	IN THE '20S	IN 1938
IN THE MID-'50S	TWO YEARS BEFORE WORLD WAR II STARTED	IN 1924
ABOUT 60 YEARS AGO	IN THE MIDDLE OF THE LAST CENTURY	IN 1916
IN 1876	ONE HUNDRED YEARS AGO TODAY	IN 1895
ALMOST 30 YEARS AGO	A FEW YEARS AFTER WORLD WAR II	IN 1960
IN THE LATE '20S	BETWEEN 1955 AND 1958	BEFORE 1880
JUST UNDER 40 YEARS AGO	DURING THE LAST DECADE OF THE 19TH CENTURY	OVER 70 YEARS AGO
ALMOST 40 YEARS AGO	IN THE MID-'30S	IN 1928

3.2

unit 3 Talking about things past

Joke go-betweens

Level
intermediate –
upper-intermediate

Class size
groups of three or four

Language focus
simple past questions/
reporting verbs *say, tell,
ask*

Pronunciation
intonation pattern in *wh-*
questions: *What did the
doctor say?*

Preparation time
10 minutes

Game time
25 minutes

Before class
Make one set of the **Jumbled jokes** (p.27) for each group of three to four learners. Familiarise yourself with the jokes so that you can answer questions about them without having to look at them written down. Cut the pieces out along the dotted lines and mix up all the pieces.

In class
1 This is a game where learners race to sort out four jumbled-up jokes by asking appropriate questions to a person who knows the jokes.

2 Divide the class into groups of three to four players. Give each group a set of the jumbled-up jokes. Tell each group to arrange its jumbled-up pieces on a desk. Explain that learners have to put the pieces in the correct order. To sort out the jokes, they will have to ask a number of questions, for example *who said what to who* or *who asked who what*. Tell learners you will be available to answer questions.

3 The aim of the game is to be the first group to sort all four jokes correctly.

4 Place yourself on a chair in the middle of the groups. Explain that to ask a question, a group must send you a 'go-between' (one member of their group). You will answer the question and the 'go-between' will report back to his/her group.

There are, however, three rules for asking questions:

a Groups can only ask you *wh-* questions: *who/where/what/why*.

b Groups can only ask questions about what was said/asked/told etc. by the characters in the jokes.

c You will only answer the question if it is grammatically correct.

If a group asks a question that is not grammatically correct, send the 'go-between' back to his/her group. Members of the groups must take it in turns to be the 'go-between'.

Example exchanges:

Group A: *Who was the woman on the train talking to?*
Teacher: *A policeman.*

Group B: *What said the man to the doctor?*
Teacher: *That's not a correct question.*

Group C: *What did the policeman answer?*
Teacher: *He said it was common.*

5 When one group thinks it has sorted out all the jokes, check their answers. If the group is right, it wins, if not, continue the game.

Jumbled jokes

A man on a train had just made some very cruel comments about how ugly he found a little child to be. The mother and the child got off at the next stop.

'Oh, I've just been terribly insulted.'

said the woman

to a nearby policeman.

'I am sorry,' he said, 'we get all sorts of complaints these days.'

'Isn't there anything you can do?'

'Not a lot,' he replied,

'but if you'd like to take a seat, I'll fetch you a cup of tea and a banana for your monkey.'

'Well, what can I do for you?'

a cannibal doctor asked his cannibal patient.

'It's my wife,'

said the patient,

'I don't like the look of her.'

'Never mind,'

advised the doctor,

'just eat the potatoes.'

A patient who had been having trouble with his arm went to see a doctor for help.

'It hurts me when I hold it like this,' he said.

'Well, don't hold it like that,'

replied the doctor.

'No, I get this pain in three places,'

the patient insisted.

'So stay away from them,'

came the answer.

A woman crept silently into her child's bedroom.

'There is a burglar in the kitchen eating all my cakes and pies,'

said the mother to the child.

'Phone for a policeman quickly,'

she whispered.

'We won't need one,'

he answered,

'I'll call a doctor.'

3.3 Last week's news

Level
pre-intermediate –
upper-intermediate

Class size
whole class

Language focus
simple past/past
continuous question forms/
question tags

Pronunciation
rise fall intonation pattern
when seeking confirmation
↘..., didn't he? ↗

Preparation time
5 minutes

Game time
30 minutes

Before class

Make one or two sample **Game cards** (explanation below) to demonstrate how the game works. In addition, think of six familiar characters who were in the news last week, e.g. TV soap characters, sports personalities. You may use these characters to prompt students as they write their cards.

*With advanced classes, you may wish to bring last week's newspapers to serve as prompts for the cards.

In class

1 This is a competitive game where teams race to be the first to find details about well-known current events.

2 Divide the class into four or five teams. Give each team about six strips of paper/card and then demonstrate what they have to write on the card, i.e. the name of a personality in large letters.

> President Clinton

On the back of the card, they need to write one true detail and something he/she did/was doing last week.

> He was touring in Asia last week.

3 The aim of the game is to be the team that wins the most cards by correctly finding out the detail written on the back of each card.

4 When each team has made five or six cards – prompt teams where necessary with the characters you thought of before class – you are ready to start the game.

Show the class the name on a sample card again. Explain that in order to win a card, learners will have to find out the 'true' detail written on the back. Thus learners have to ask questions to try to confirm a fact that they think they already know. For example:

> Chung Fee Ming

Didn't he buy a new pet last week?
or *He bought a new pet last week, didn't he?*

If you are using this game to practise question tags, stress that the questions must finish with a *did/didn't he/she? was/wasn't he/she?*

To start: teams take it in turns to hold up a card, showing the name of the personality. Players from other teams should then shout out questions in a race to win the card.

5 If a question does not correspond to the detail on the card, the player with the card says *I'm afraid I don't know*. If the question does match the detail, the team wins the card. The team with the most cards at the end of the game is the winner.

unit 3 Talking about things past

Past identities

3.4

Before class
Collect or ask learners to bring a prop or clothes accessory (one per learner) e.g. a wig, patch, pipe, headband etc. Also – or alternatively – give each learner the title and chorus line of a well-known song.

In class
1 This is a game of 'remembering by association'.

2 Divide the class into groups of four or six learners. Ask each learner to write down five questions to ask members of other groups. The questions should be *wh-/how* questions and not more than six words long. For example:

My questions	Names of answerers
1 How old are you?	
2 Where were you born?	

Now ask learners to take their prop and/or memorise the line of their song.

3 The aim of the game is to be the group with the highest number of correctly-remembered identities of people who have asked questions.

4 Now ask learners to mingle (whole class) and ask each of their questions to two other people (not members of their own group). After getting an answer, the 'asker' should sing the line of his/her song (if included in the game). The asker should also note down the names of the learners who answered the question. For example, Piet writes:

My questions	Names of answerers
1 How old are you?	Yoko François
2 Where were you born?	Hans Cécile

After asking their questions, learners return to their groups and remove their accessories. Each learner writes his or her name on his/her own question sheet, and puts it in a group pile.

Now nominate one member of a group to choose a question sheet at random from the group pile. For example, using Piet's sheet (above) Fausto might ask:

Yoko, who asked you how old you are/were?

Yoko now tries to answer by saying *what he was wearing/holding* etc. and/or *singing*.

5 Keep group scores on the board: one point for every detail correctly remembered. Groups take it in turns to ask questions.

Level
pre-intermediate –
intermediate

Class size
groups of four to six

Language focus
use of past continuous for background detail, description

Pronunciation
weak form: *was* /wəz/
linking: *who_asked*

Preparation time
10 minutes

Game time
30 minutes

4.1

Level
pre-intermediate

Class size
groups of four or five

Language focus
comparative
adjectives, adverbs
taller than, as big as

Pronunciation
weak forms:
than /ðən/ as /əz/

Preparation time
5 minutes

Game time
25 minutes

unit 4 Making comparisons

Line up accordingly

Before class

Make one copy of the **Line-up commands** (p.31) and cut the commands out as cards so that they can be given separately to different groups of learners. Also, make one or two copies of the **Question prompts sheet** (p.31) to give each group of learners to look at during the game.

*If you have a mixed nationality class, you can give learners prompts that relate to their different countries e.g. size of country etc.

In class

1 This is a game where groups line up in order according to particular commands that they are given and other groups have to deduce what the command was.

2 Divide the class into three or four groups with about four or five learners in each. Explain that groups will be asked to line up according to a command they are given and the other groups will have to work out what the line-up represents by asking questions. Give each group two or three of the Line-up command cards that you cut up before class. Also give each group a **Question prompts sheet** that will help members to think of possible questions during the game.

3 The aim of the game is to be the group that has made the highest number of deductions of what the line-ups represent.

4 Nominate one group to line up first. After studying one of their Line-up cards, the group should line up accordingly, from left to right: i.e. most to least (e.g. tallest to shortest). If, in any round, two or more learners are the same, e.g. the same shoe size, this should be reflected in the line-up as follows:

Fabienne   Rico   Karl   Amy   Judith

with the learners who are the same lining up closer together.

Learners from other groups now have to ask questions to work out what the line-up represents. The questions must be asked to a particular individual and must involve a **comparative form**. Learners should ask questions of a different member of the line-up each time (i.e. not keep asking the same person questions). If the question is irrelevant, learners should answer 'I don't know'. For example, using the line-up above:

Learner: *Fabienne, are you older than Rico?*
Fabienne: *I don't know* (because the group is not lining up according to age).
Learner: *Rico, is your family larger than Karl's?*
Rico: *I don't know* (because the group is not lining up according to family size) etc.

After every two questions, write up one word of the target question on the board, so that gradually the questions become more focused e.g. *Do you have ...*

5 The first group to get the correct detail by asking the right question is given the Line-up command card, and the group with the most cards at the end wins.

Line-up commands   **Target questions**

| LINE UP ACCORDING TO **AGE.** |

◀ *Are you older than … ?*

| LINE UP ACCORDING TO **SHOE SIZE.** |

◀ *Do you have larger feet than … ?*

| LINE UP ACCORDING TO **SIZE OF FAMILY.** |

◀ *Is your family larger than … ?*

| LINE UP ACCORDING TO DISTANCE OF **JOURNEY TO SCHOOL.** |

◀ *Is your journey to school longer than … ?*

| LINE UP ACCORDING TO **LENGTH OF HAIR.** |

◀ *Is your hair longer than … ?*

| LINE UP ACCORDING TO **100 M TIME.** |

◀ *Do you have a faster 100 m time than … ?*

| LINE UP ACCORDING TO **LENGTH OF YOUR NAME.** |

◀ *Is your name longer than … ?*

| LINE UP ACCORDING TO **TIME YOU GET UP.** |

◀ *Do you get up earlier than … ?*

| LINE UP ACCORDING TO **HOW FAR YOU WERE BORN FROM SCHOOL.** |

◀ *Were you born further from the school than … ?*

Question prompts sheet

TIME	HEIGHT	NAME	HANDS
MORNING	FAMILY	HAIR	FEET
CLOTHES	BIRTHDAY	ENGLISH	HOUSE
DISTANCE	EYES	JOURNEY	PETS
WEIGHT	MATHS	HANDWRITING	FINGERNAILS

4.2 Psychic partners

Level
intermediate

Class size
groups of four

Language focus
superlative adjectives and adverbs

Pronunciation
linking: *most_exciting,
most_unusual*

Preparation time
5 minutes

Game time
30 minutes

Before class
Make one copy of each of the **Question prompt lists** (p.33) for each group of four learners.

In class
1 This is a game based on a popular TV quiz played in many countries based on how well you know your partner.

2 Put learners into groups of four. Divide each group of four into two pairs (A and B). Give each pair one of the **Question prompt lists** and ask them not to show it to the other pair. Ask learners to turn the question prompts into full questions that will then be put to learners in another group.

Explain to learners, however, that when they put a question to another person then that question will be about that person's partner. For example,

| choose / attractive actor or actress? | *Who would she (i.e. your partner) choose as the most attractive actor?* a .... b .... c .... |

Also explain that, as above, the questions must make use of a superlative form and give the learner a multiple-choice (a b c) set of answers to choose from.

3 The aim of the game is to be the pair that gives the highest number of corresponding answers to the questions which are put to learners individually.

4 Before learners write the question prompts as full questions, make sure that they understand that they will be playing the game against the other pair in their group of four.

There are 12 questions on each prompt sheet. When pairs have finished writing their questions out in full, ask learners to change partners in their groups of four. Thus, John and Yoko would change partners with Raoul and Catalina. John will ask Raoul six of the 12 questions, and vice versa; and Yoko will ask Catalina the other six questions and vice versa. For example:

John: *Raoul, who would Catalina* (Raoul's original partner) *choose as the most attractive actress?* a .... b .... c ....

Make sure that when you put learners from different pairs together they will be far enough away from their original partner so as not to be able to hear what he/she is being asked/answering.

When the questions have been asked and the answers noted, all four learners should get together in one group. Learners now put the same questions to the other member of the opposing pair, and discover if the preferences cited by one partner were in fact correct predictions. Thus, John now asks Catalina directly for her preferences:

John: *Catalina, who would you choose as the most attractive actor?* a .... b .... c ....

5 A pair scores one point for every answer that was correctly predicted, and the winner of the game is the pair with the most points after all the answers have been checked.

Question prompt lists

Pair A

choose /attractive actor or actress?

say / be / film of year?

choose / gifted musician?

likely / order / eat / restaurant?

say / colour / suits him or her?

say / programme / most /on TV?

. . . .

choose / exciting / sports star?

say / good record / charts now?

choose / good place / holiday?

say / difficult subject / school?

choose / desirable car?

choose / good animal / have / pet?

Pair B

choose / funny / comedian?

say / good place / go with friends?

choose / bad programme / on TV?

say / colour / suits him or her?

say / subject / like / school?

say / take him or her / long / mornings?

. . . .

choose / exciting / sport?

say / good way / relax?

soft drink / likely order / café?

say / job / like / in the future?

say / good film / cinema / at moment?

choose / attractive TV personality?

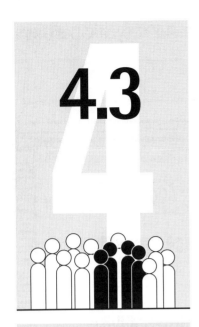

4.3 Comparative short straws

Before class

Make one set each of the **Straw cards A** and **B** (p.35) and one **Key** for each pair of learners. Pair A will be playing the game against Pair B who will have the other set of 'straw' cards(**B**).

In class

1 This game is based on the idea of drawing straws when someone needs to be selected to do something. 'Drawing the short straw' from a bunch of long straws is what participants try to avoid.

2 Put learners into pairs and arrange the class so that Pair A is facing Pair B. Give each pair the relevant set of **Straw cards**, which they should put face-down in front of them.

Each card has two 'items' and the first two 'letters' of the third item.
All the items are from the same category. For example:

> **Length:**
> First World War   Second World War   Vi ...

If the heading on the top of the card relates to 'Length'; two of the three items will be roughly the same; one of the three, however, will be much longer/shorter than the other two.

Where the third item is much longer, the card is a long straw.
Where the third item is much shorter, the card is a short straw.

Thus the card above is a long straw because the Vietnam War was much longer than the other two. The fact that 'Vi' stands for 'Vietnam' will not be revealed until the end of the game.

3 The aim of the game is to collect as many long straw cards as you can and reject all the short straws.

4 Each pair should place their pile of straw cards face-down in front of them. Each round begins by both pairs turning over the top card in their pile. Each pair now discusses whether or not they want to keep their card.

If they want to keep it, they put it to one side until the end of the game: if not, the other pair have the chance to keep it. If they don't want it either, the card is put on a reject pile and a new round begins.

At the end of the game, therefore, each team is left with a pile of cards that they believe to be long straws.

5 Now give each pair a copy of the **Key** so they can see how many long straws they have. The winning pair is the one with the most long straws, but every short straw cancels out a long one.

Level
upper-intermediate

Class size
groups of four

Language focus
much longer, far shorter, just as large as ..., roughly the same as ...

Pronunciation
weak forms: *just /dʒəst/ as /əz/*
linking: *just‿as/same‿as*

Preparation time
5 minutes

Game time
20 minutes

Straw cards A

> **Length:**
> First World War   Second World War   Vi ...

> **How long ago discovered by Europeans:**
> North America   Australia   Ne ...

> **Length, men's world record:**
> hammer   discus   ja ...

> **Length of match:**
> football   hockey   bo ...

> **Length of journey to mainland:**
> Sicily   Hong Kong   Cu ...

> **Length of time since invented:**
> radio   X-rays   te ...

> **Average length of life:**
> cat   dog   bu ...

> **Length of longest border:**
> Norway   Belgium   Sw ...

Straw cards B

> **Length of time since invented:**
> frozen food   talking pictures   mi ...

> **Length of longest border:**
> Portugal   Spain   Ch ...

> **Length of journey to sea:**
> Tokyo   Paris   Mo ...

> **Length of time since independence:**
> Algeria   Malaysia   Un ...

> **Length:**
> Nile   London Thames   Am ...

> **Length of longest:**
> alligator   blue whale   sn ...

> **Length of alphabet:**
> English   Chinese   Gr ...

> **Length:**
> metre   yard   in ...

Key

A	**Vi**etnam (long straw); **Ne**w Zealand (long straw: North America); **ja**velin (long straw); **bo**xing (short straw); **Cu**ba (long straw); **te**lephone (long straw); **bu**tterfly (short straw); **Sw**eden (short straw: Belgium).
B	**mi**crochip (short straw); **Ch**ile (long straw); **Mo**scow (long straw); **Un**ited States (long straw); **Am**azon (London Thames: short straw); **sn**ake (blue whale: long straw); **Gr**eek (Chinese long straw); **in**ch (short straw).

4.4 Ratio roulette

Before class

Take to class one copy (perhaps on OHT) of the **Comparisons list** below.

In class

1 This is a general knowledge game involving speculation about number and size.

2 Divide learners into groups of three and ask one of the learners in each group to write the following ratios on a piece of paper.

> 1:1 1:2 1:3 etc. up to 1:10.

On the board (or using an OHT) write the following **Comparisons list**:

number of rows on a chess board/ number of squares on a chess board	Paris, distance from London/ Athens, distance from London
age of Aztec pyramid temples/ age of Egyptian pyramids	number of countries bordering Spain/ number of countries bordering the US
number of circles in Olympic flag/ number of circles in Japanese flag	population, London/ population, Mexico City
world's tallest/shortest man	world's highest waterfall/ world's highest mountain
oldest snake/oldest man	one mile/sixteen kilometres

3 Explain to the class that they have to discuss in their groups how big the difference is between the comparisons and match the comparison to the appropriate ratio on their piece of paper. They should also write a sentence expressing the ratio/comparison. For example:

> 1:3   World's tallest/shortest man
> The world's tallest man is three times as
> tall as the world's shortest man.

4 The winner of the game is the group that gets the highest number of answers in the correct ratio slots.

Key:		(Answers)
1:1	countries bordering Spain/US	(Portugal, France/Mexico, Canada);
1:2	London/Mexico City pop.	(8.5 million/17 million);
1:3	oldest snake/oldest man	(40 years/120 years);
1:4	world's shortest/tallest man	(65 cm/2.72 m);
1:5	circles, Olympic flag/Japanese flag	(five and one);
1:6	distance Paris/Athens	(250/1,500 miles);
1:7	age of Aztec/Egyptian pyramids	(750 years/4,500 years):
1:8	rows/squares on a chess board	(8/64);
1:9	height, waterfall/mountain	(1,000 m – Salto Angelo, Venezuela; Everest – 9,000 m);
1:10	one mile/16 km	(1,600 m = one mile)

Level
intermediate

Class size
groups of three

Language focus
twice/three times as big, costs twice as much, much larger etc

Pronunciation
'schwa' sound: *as* /əz/ *than* /ðən/

Preparation time
2 minutes

Game time
20 minutes

Sort yourselves out

5.1

Before class

Write each of the words in the example sentences below on a separate piece of paper/card. Keep the words in their respective sentences, but jumbled up, and bound together with a paper clip/elastic band.

Elementary sentences:

We often go to Saturday matches.
I like my school very much.
We are learning English very quickly.
We are going home tomorrow morning.
My friend often travels to Germany.
He is always asking silly questions.
I am only staying here until tomorrow.
My basketball team lost badly yesterday.
You can always come here later.
We usually get a bus home after school.
They are often a little early.
We don't always work well together.

Intermediate – upper-intermediate sentences:

We only just made it home in time.
I don't even go there much any more.
She always wears boots, even in summer.
It still hasn't got here yet.

I worked hard at home all day yesterday.
He drove unusually slowly all the way here.
She can't seriously have minded going alone.
It got here incredibly quickly last week.

She probably went to bed early last night.
They must have both been badly hurt.

You mustn't move around the house at all.
She nearly always loses her temper.

In class

1 This is a game played as a race, involving teams of several learners lining up.

2 Divide the class into two or three teams, depending on the size of the class (six to nine members per team).

In order to have maximum involvement, the number of words in a sentence should approximate the number of members of a team (but this is not a vital condition for the activity's success!). Extra team members may work as pairs.

3 Arrange the class so that one member of each team stands in the middle of the other team members, ready to give out the words in the sentence. For each round of the game, you can either give teams the same sentence, or different sentences. When you say *go*, the team member in the middle gives out one word to each team member.

Team members must then line themselves up as quickly as possible in order to make a correctly-ordered sentence. They signal that they have completed their sentence by holding the words above their heads.

4 If they are right, they win the round; if not, say *no* and the race continues until one team has sorted itself into a correct sentence. The team that wins the most rounds is the winner.

Level
elementary –
upper-intermediate

Class size
whole class

Language focus
position/order of adverbs in
the sentence

Pronunciation
intonation: continuing fall
– rise pattern, closing fall
pattern: *He probably went
to bed early last night.*

Preparation time
15 minutes

Game time
25 minutes

Level
pre-intermediate –
intermediate

Class size
groups of three

Language focus
order of adjectives before
the noun

Pronunciation
fall–rise intonation (lists):
*a tall, dark, handsome
stranger*

Preparation time
10 minutes

Game time
25 minutes

unit 5 Describing things

Four-card adjectives

Before class
Make one copy of the **Four-card adjectives playing cards** (p.39) and one set of the **Noun picture sheet** (p.39) for each group of three learners.

In class
1 This game is similar to a number of common card games where players pick up and throw away a card each time it is their turn.

2 Divide the class into groups of three and sit each group of three players around a noun picture sheet.

Give each group one deck of cards. Nominate one player to shuffle all the cards and deal four cards to each player (face-down). Put the remaining cards face-down in a pile except for the top one which should remain face-up next to the pile.

3 The aim of the game is to get a run of four cards (adjectives) that can come before one of the pictures (nouns). For example, a

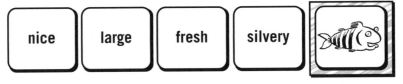

4 Tell the class that each player must take it in turns to pick up and throw away a card. They can either pick up a card from the pack or the last card that the previous player threw away. They may throw away any card from their own hand, or even the card they have picked up.

When a player thinks he/she has a run of four cards, he/she puts his/her cards down in front of the appropriate picture on the board.

If the other players agree that the noun can be described that way and that the adjectives are in the right order, the player wins the round. This picture cannot be used in subsequent rounds. All cards are shuffled and dealt again.

In cases where there is disagreement about a run, the teacher should act as judge. If a player is found to have put his/her hand down incorrectly, he/she takes back the cards and misses his or her next turn.

5 The winner of the game is the first player to win three rounds.

Four-card adjectives playing cards

long	cold	refreshing	fizzy
fashionable	long	baggy	Italian
nice	large	fresh	silvery
long	curved	exotic	sandy
funny	little	old	black
new	knee-length	shiny	leather
great	new	action-packed	Hollywood
exciting	new	young	Chinese

5.3 Collocation bridges

Before class
Make one copy of the **Collocation bridge puzzle** (p.41) for each pair of learners.

In class

1 This is a puzzle game where learners have to put words into a correct pattern of opposites and collocates to progress around a game board.

2 To give learners the idea of finding words which collocate or bond together, write the following on the blackboard:

fair   rain
even   ⌐ result
light   └ numbers

and ask learners to match one word from the left column to one on the right.

3 The aim of the game is to be the first pair to successfully build a bridge from the starting point to the finishing point on the puzzle board.

4 Put learners into pairs. Explain that players need to choose words from around the edge of the board and put them in their correct position so that they bond with other words in the following way:

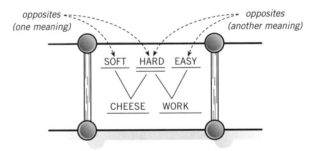

There is only one correct way of organising all the words to build a bridge successfully to get to the other side. Adjectives should be placed in opposite pairs around the outside edge of the 'bridge'; nouns on the inside edge.

Explain that the game is a race. When learners think they are over the bridge, they should shout: 'Over' and read the words out that make their bridge, for example: heavy rain light rain light colours dark colours etc.

5 If the pair is correct, it wins; if not, you say: 'In the water' and the game starts again from the point where the error occurred. Pairs can only read out their answers for a second time once another pair has had a turn.

Key:
odd place   ordinary place   odd numbers   even numbers
light colours   dark colours   light rain   heavy rain
poor countries   rich countries   poor results   good results
smart clothes   casual clothes   smart decision   stupid decision
smooth skin   rough skin   rough child   gentle child
easy job   tough job   tough meat   tender meat
lively concert   dull concert   dull weather   bright weather

---

Level
intermediate –
upper-intermediate

Class size
pairs

Language focus
adjectival opposites/
noun-adjective collocation

Pronunciation
contrastive stress: even
numbers/odd numbers

Preparation time
5 minutes

Game time
15–20 minutes

Collocation bridge puzzle

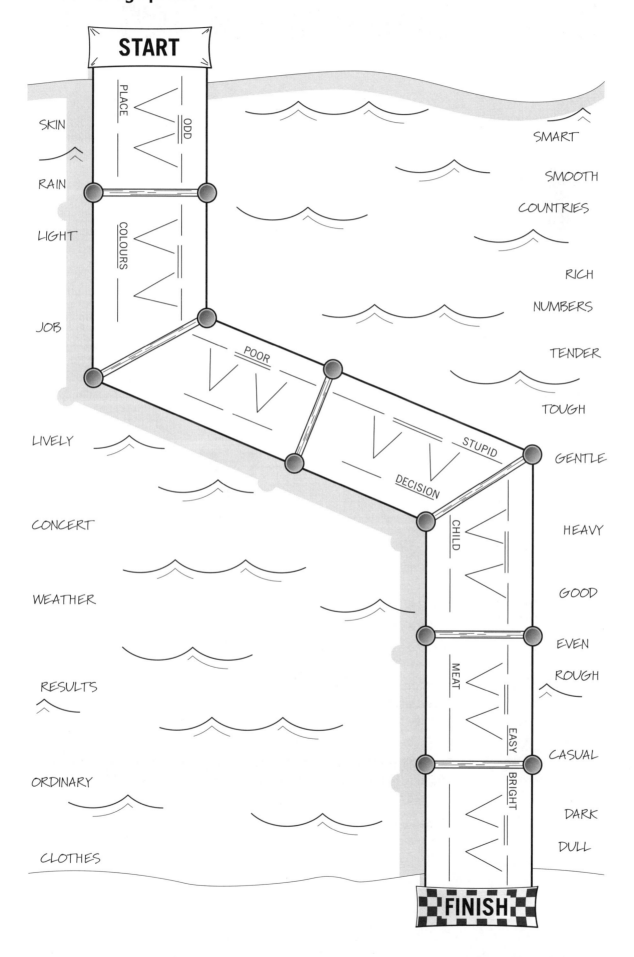

5.4 Square routes

Before class
Make one copy of the **Square routes game board** (p.43) and one copy of both sets of counters (p.43) for every four members of the class.

In class
1 This is a board game where learners move counters from the centre to the edge of the board. Making a move means making a grammatical choice.

2 Divide learners into pairs and seat two pairs around one game board. Give one pair the plain counters and the other pair the shaded counters.

3 The aim of the game is to be the first pair to get its counters off the board.

4 Explain to learners that they start with all their counters in the centre of the board. Each pair takes it in turn to move a counter into an adjoining square into which the counter fits grammatically. For example, a pair playing their GOOD counter in this position can only move it forward because it does not fit into either of the adjoining squares.

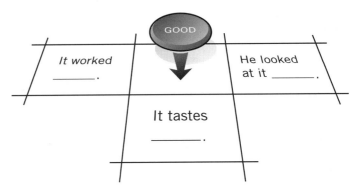

If Pair A makes a move that Pair B feels is incorrect, it may be challenged by Pair B. If the move is agreed to be wrong (possibly after adjudication by the teacher) the counter stays where it is, and Pair A misses its turn.

A situation of deadlock may arise, whereby a pair finds itself grounded on a square where there appears to be no way of moving on. In this case, the pair may use the turn to move back to where it came from, even if this means returning to the START area.

Each pair starts by moving one of its counters into any of the squares adjoining the START area. A pair cannot, however, move on to a square that is already occupied by a counter.

5 When a pair successfully moves into a shaded square at the edge of the board, they may take off a counter. The winner is the first pair to get all its counters off the board.

Level
pre-intermediate – intermediate

Class size
groups of four

Language focus
use of adjectives and adverbs

Pronunciation
linking:
good_at/he's_easily/
look_easy/nice_easy

Preparation time
5 minutes

Game time
25 minutes

Square routes game board

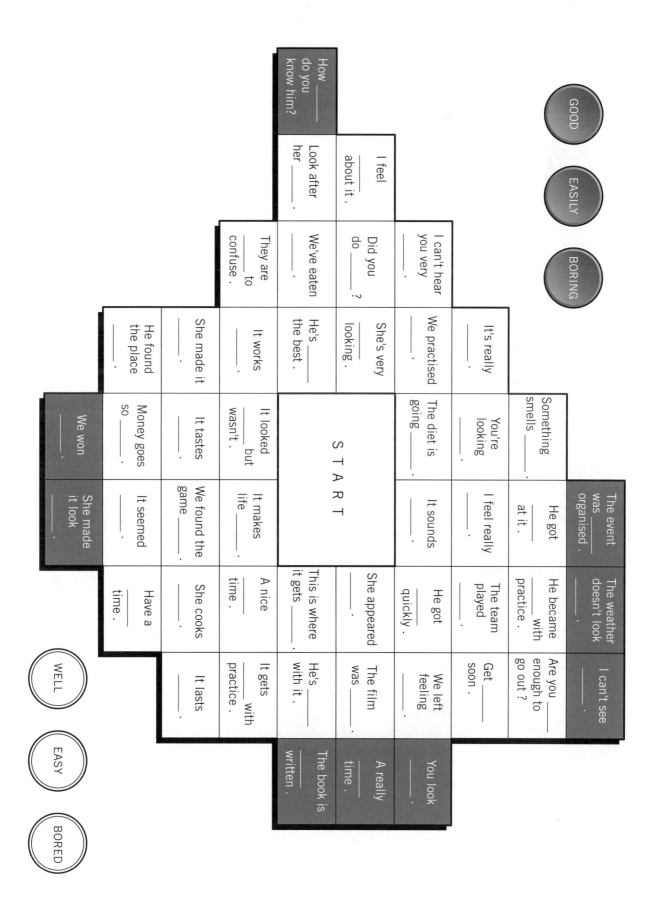

The cells of the game board read:

- How do you ____ know him?
- Look after her ____ .
- I feel ____ about it .
- I can't hear you very ____ .
- They are ____ to confuse .
- We've eaten ____ .
- Did you do ____ ?
- She's very ____ looking .
- We practised ____ .
- It's really ____ .
- He found the place ____ .
- She made it ____ .
- It works ____ .
- He's the best ____ .
- Something smells ____ .
- You're looking ____ .
- The diet is going ____ .
- We won ____ .
- Money goes so ____ .
- It tastes ____ .
- It looked ____ but wasn't .
- S T A R T
- I feel really ____ .
- The event was organised ____ .
- She made it look ____ .
- It seemed ____ .
- We found the game ____ .
- It makes life ____ .
- This is where it gets ____ .
- She appeared ____ .
- It sounds ____ .
- He got ____ at it .
- He got ____ quickly .
- The weather doesn't look ____ .
- Have a ____ time .
- She cooks ____ .
- A nice ____ time .
- It gets ____ with it .
- He's ____ with it .
- The film was ____ .
- The team played ____ .
- He became ____ with practice .
- Get ____ soon .
- We left feeling ____ .
- Are you ____ enough to go out ?
- I can't see ____ .
- It lasts ____ .
- It gets ____ with practice .
- You look ____ .
- A really ____ time .
- The book is ____ written .

Counters: GOOD, EASILY, BORING, WELL, EASY, BORED

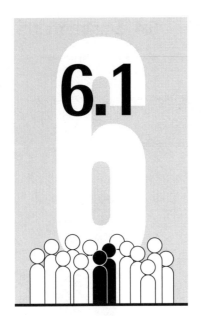

6.1

Arrangement squares

Before class

Make one copy of the **Diary grid** (p.45) for each member of class and one copy of the **Activity cards** (also p.45) for each pair of learners. Cut the **Activity cards** out and put them into separate piles ('player X' and 'player O').

In class

1 This activity is like an extended game of Noughts (O) and Crosses (X).

2 Put learners into pairs and explain that each person will be playing the game against his/her partner. Give each learner a **Diary grid** and one set of 'player X' or 'player O' cards. The cards should be placed face-down as it is important that the players do not see them. Then ask players to look at their cards. Explain that they should write down on the **Diary grid** when they plan to do each activity, and also write on the dotted line when they plan to do the activity.

Players should only write each activity once on their grid so that 12 slots in the **Diary grid** are taken up and all the other slots represent times when they are free. In each pair, one player is Noughts (O) and the other Crosses (X) for the purposes of the game.

3 The aim of the game is for players to put as many Noughts or Crosses on the board (the **Diary grid**) as they can, and to try and get as many lines of three Noughts or Crosses as possible.

4 Players should take it in turns to ask the opponent for help, to join them, accompany them etc. in one of the activities marked in their grid. So, for example, Player (X) asks, '*Can you help me wash the car on Tuesday afternoon?*' And Player (O) can now answer in one of three ways, for example: '*OK, I'm not doing anything,*' if Player (O) has no activity on that square already. In which case, both players mark this square with an 'X' on the grid; '*Sorry, I can't, I'm going shopping,*' if Player (O) already has an activity on the square. If Player (X) believes this answer, both players mark this square with an 'O'. Thirdly, Player (O) can lie (to try and win another square) by offering some fictitious excuse: '*I'm sorry I can't, I'm going to the library*'. If Player (X) accepts this, then both players mark this square with an 'O'.

If, however, Player (X) challenges: '*I don't believe you*', Player (O) has to produce the card with the activity (plus correct time) on it. If Player (O) produces the card, not only do both players mark O on the square in question, but Player (O) also nominates another square where O should be put. If Player (O) cannot produce the card, then an X is marked on the square in question, and Player (X) nominates another square where an X is to be put.

5 The game ends when both players have asked for help etc. with all their activities. The aim of the game is to be the player at the end who has the most lines of three Os or Xs (horizontal, vertical or diagonal).

Level
pre-intermediate

Class size
pairs

Language focus
use of present continuous to talk about future arrangements

Pronunciation
I'm /aɪm/
weak forms: *can* /kən/
you /jə/

Preparation time
10 minutes

Game time
20 minutes

Diary grid

	MORNING	AFTERNOON	EVENING
Monday			
Tuesday			
Wednesday			
Thursday			
Friday			
Saturday			

Activity cards

Player X

parachute practice

ice-skating

Japanese lesson

guitar lesson

a wedding

shopping

take cat to vet

Grandfather's birthday party

an exam

skiing

hairdresser's

tennis

Player O

football match

go to gym

ballet

wash the car

aerobics

beach

school trip

acting classes

circus

fishing

hospital

dentist's

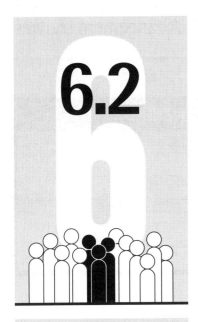

6.2 Pantomime fish

Level
pre-intermediate –
intermediate

Class size
groups of three of four

Language focus
use of *will*: offers,
promises, predictions,
spontaneous decisions

Pronunciation
contraction: *I'll* /aɪl/
weak form: *be* /bɪ/

Preparation time
10 minutes

Game time
25 minutes

Before class

Make one copy of the **'Will'sheet** (p.47) to copy on to the board or on to an OHT. Before starting the activity, ask learners in groups of three or four to copy each offer/promise/prediction etc. on to a separate strip of paper, so that each group has one set of the responses.

You may also wish to practise the monologue, **The fish story**, on p.47 before going to class so that you are familiar with it when reading it to the class. You may also want to pre-teach some of the vocabulary.

In class

1 Introduce the class to the idea of the pantomime and how the audience usually 'participates', i.e. offers encouragement or advice to the actors, e.g. *He's behind you.*

Explain that you have something to tell them, but that – as in a pantomime – you may need a little support or encouragement, because some parts of what you have to say may be a little sad or embarrassing.

2 Divide the class into groups (A, B, C etc.) of three or four. Ask learners to arrange the strips of paper in front of them so that everyone in the group can see them. If you have already looked at these uses of 'will' in class, you might like to get learners to discuss in their groups when they might say these things, i.e. which ones are promises, predictions, offers, etc. Seat the groups so that you can move between them freely as you read your monologue.

3 The aim of the game for groups is to try to have as few strips of paper remaining as possible on conclusion of the reading of the monologue.

4 Ask students to arrange their strips of paper in front of them so that they can get to them easily and explain that when there is an opportunity in your story to provide encouragement, offer help, etc. using one of the phrases, they should shout it out. If their promise, offer, prediction etc. is appropriate you will go to the team and take the strip of paper from them. If it is not appropriate, you simply continue with your story.

Use long pauses and repetition in your monologue if it takes the class a little time to get used to the game.

5 When you have finished telling your story, the group that has given you the most encouragement (strips of paper) wins the game. You may then wish to tell it again, repeating the process.

'Will' sheet

You'll be okay!	We'll help!	We'll do that.
He won't know.	He won't mind!	He will!
He'll be alright!	We won't tell!	I'll remind you.
I'll find out for you ...	He'll wait.	I'll get you one!

The FISH story

I'm going to the hospital today ... I'm a bit worried actually, because I'm going to see a friend who's been ill ... The doctor says that he can come home now but he needs someone to stay with him ... I can spend some time with him, but I'm busy teaching, you know ...

Anyway, I'm going to bring him home on the bus. I haven't got enough money for a taxi ... I hope that's OK with him ... I've never been to the hospital before, I hope I don't get lost ... I'm terrible with directions ... Really, I am ... I don't know about the bus times either ... I've got so much to do before I leave, I'll never get it all done ...

Anyway I was talking about my friend ... He wants to keep his illness a secret ... It is funny though ... but perhaps I shouldn't say anything ... but it is funny ... no, I shouldn't ... oh, alright then ...

Well, he went into hospital last week and some of the best doctors in the country came to see him. At first they were very confused about what the problem was. He had all sorts of tests but it took three days and four doctors to find the problem ...

Oh, I don't know if I've got the time to tell you the whole story, I'll be late ...

I need to take the dog for a walk before I go ... and get some shopping ...

He won't like me telling people about his problem ... Oh, I suppose it's alright ...

Well, when the doctors came to see him again, they asked him to sit down.
'We have some bad news', they said. All four doctors said together, 'You have: FISH'.

'Fish,' he said confused. 'Yes,' they all replied ...

I think he'll be pleased to see me ... I've bought these flowers, I hope he likes them ... I didn't get any chocolates ... because I'm not sure what he can eat ... I do hope he gets better soon ... I suppose his house needs cleaning too ... Oh, and I mustn't forget to take his keys ...

Anyway, where was I ... oh yes: 'Flu,' said the first doctor. 'Indigestion,' said the second.

'Spots,' said the third, and 'Hay Fever,' said the fourth. 'FISH,' they all repeated together.

'Oh, no,' said my friend, 'what am I going to do?'

He's never been ill before, I am worried ...

I may need a tissue ... because I might start crying when I see him ...

Oh, and I should take the hospital phone number with me in case I get lost ...

I forgot to water his plants yesterday ...
I ought to water them now I suppose ... I mustn't be late ... He could be ready to leave now ...

Well anyway, he asked the doctors what they were going to do.

'Oh dear, dear, dear ... Flu, Indigestion, Spots and Hay Fever, ... dear me ... FISH ... horrible,' said one of the doctors.

'We're going to keep you here in hospital and put you on a diet of thin wafer biscuits and cheese slices,' he added.

'Thin wafer biscuits and cheese slices ... will that help?' asked my friend.

'I don't know,' replied the doctor, 'but it's the only thing we'll be able to pass under the door.'

6.3

Collecting evidence

unit 6 Looking to the future

Before class

Make one large set of the **Evidence cards** and one set of the **Person cards** (both on p. 49). You may wish to write these out on card in large letters as they will need to be stuck to the board so that the whole class can see them. On the back of the **Person cards** write the accompanying predictions (see p. 49).

In class

1 This is a game where learners have to speculate about what certain characters might say, given certain evidence.

2 Stick all the **Evidence cards** and **Person cards** ('person' side showing) randomly on the board:

the score is 6–6   cinema-goer   best friend
parent   there's fog and ice

Divide the class into three to five teams (roughly four members per team). Explain to the class that on the back of each **Person card** there is a prediction based on one of the pieces of evidence stuck somewhere else on the board.

3 The aim of the game is to try and guess as many of the predictions as possible based on the evidence.

4 What teams have to do is look at the board and try to match a **Person card** to one of the **Evidence cards**. When they think they have a match, one member of the team runs and tells it to you. If he/she is correct, he/she takes the **Evidence card** (not the **Person card**) and returns to the team with it. If he/she is wrong, he/she returns to the team and tries again.

When all the **Evidence cards** have been taken by the teams, you can begin the next stage of the game. Nominate one team to start by telling the class which 'person' on the board their **Evidence card** goes with. For example:

*We think our card **There's a traffic jam** goes with **the driver**.*

This team now has the first opportunity to guess what the prediction is on the back of the **Person card** (based on the evidence they are holding). For example:

*We think he's saying: **I'm going to be late!***

If they are right, they win the **Person card**. If not, the first team to shout out the correct prediction wins the **Person card**.

5 The team with most **Person cards** at the end of the game wins. Alternatively, you may like to use a different scoring system, giving one point for every grammatically correct prediction, and three points when a team guesses what is on the back of the card.

Level
pre-intermediate

Class size
whole class

Language focus
use of *be going to*: predictions based on present evidence

Pronunciation
weak forms: *to* /tə/ *be* /bɪ/

Preparation time
10 minutes

Game time
25 minutes

Evidence cards

Evidence cards	Person cards
The sea is very rough.	ship passenger
There's a traffic jam.	driver
It's dark and cloudy.	weatherman
It's a penalty!	football fan
The lights are going out!	cinema-goer
There's fog and ice.	air traveller
The score is 6–6.	tennis fan
Someone is going away for six months.	best friend
There's no wind at all.	kite-flyer
The needle is touching 'empty'.	car passenger
Children are outside in winter with no coats.	parent
Instructions: do not use pen.	pupil

Predictions to write on the back of the Person cards:

ship passenger:	I'm going to be sick!
driver:	I'm going to be late!
weatherman:	It's going to rain.
football fan:	He's going to score!
cinema-goer:	The film's going to start.
air traveller:	We're going to be delayed!
tennis fan:	There's going to be a tie-break!
best friend:	I'm going to miss you.
kite-flyer:	It's not going to fly.
car passenger:	We're going to need some petrol.
parent:	They are going to catch a cold.
pupil:	I'm going to need a pencil.

From **The Grammar Activity Book** by Bob Obee © Cambridge University Press 1999 **PHOTOCOPIABLE** 49

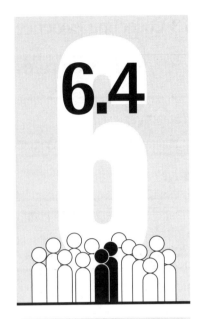

6.4 Dedication poem

Level
intermediate –
upper-intermediate

Class size
pairs

Language focus
use of *will* and other
tenses with temporal
clauses

Pronunciation
weak form: *as* /əz/
contraction: *I'll* /aɪl/

Preparation time
5 minutes

Game time
25 minutes

Before class
Make one copy of the **Poem sheet** below for each pair of learners.
This activity can also be done with other types of clauses, such as concession
clauses, e.g. *although/even though/no matter what* etc. if you wish to make a
different sheet.

In class
1 If you use the context described below, elicit from learners some of the
things you might do for a good friend. If you choose to use another context
for the poem sheet, elicit and explore the theme in a similar way.

2 Put learners into pairs. Give out the poem to each pair. Ask learners to
complete the poem in either a serious or comical way. *Timeless*, for example,
completed seriously, should produce a poem about devotion; completed
comically, it might produce a poem about all the things a person might do
for himself/herself before he/she 'is there for' his friend, parent etc.

3 The aim of the activity is to reinforce the use of the present and perfect
forms in the subordinate clause and the use of *will* in the main clause in
sentences like these. Reading out the poems and possibly displaying them
in class will help to reinforce this language point.

Example poem:

> Whenever I have nothing to do,
> As soon as my programme is over,
> After I've read this book,
> Before Christmas comes,
> The moment I find the time,
> When my diary is empty,
> Until the dog needs a walk,
> And as long as you ring first,
> I'll be there for you.

Poem sheet:

> Timeless
> Whenever _____
> As soon as _____
> After _____
> Before _____
> The moment _____
> When _____
> Until _____
> And as long as _____
> I'll be there for you.

Point in a story

7.1

Before class

Make a list of eight stories that you are sure learners in the class will know. These can be stories of any kind: the latest films, soap operas, fairytales, classic adventures. If you are unsure which stories the class will know, you could elicit eight stories from the class at the start of the game.

In class

1 This is a deduction game where learners have to race to find out the point in a story that someone else is thinking of.

2 Divide the class into four groups. Assign two of the stories to each group. Ask each member of the group to be one of the main characters in each story and to imagine a point in the story where something has just happened to them. For example, if the story were Pinnochio:

I have just grown a donkey tail. (character: Pinnochio)

Ask learners to put this information on a card/piece of paper with the name of the character written in large letters on the front and the detail on the back. When everyone has finished their cards, you are ready to begin the game.

3 The aim of the game is to be the first group to find the correct detail written on the back of the opposing groups' cards.

4 Nominate a player from one group to hold up a card with their character on it. Members from the other groups ask *yet/already* questions to try and identify the point in the story on the back of the card. For example:

Have you seen the whale yet? (ans: no)
Have you already met Stromboli? (ans: yes)

Any member from any of the other groups can shout out a question. As soon as a group gets the right answer: *Have you got donkey ears/tail yet?* (ans: *that's just happened*) they win the card for their group. One player from the next group then holds up a card and so on.

5 The group with the most cards at the end is the winner. If any card proves too difficult to find, simply move on to another card.

Level
pre-intermediate –
intermediate

Class size
whole class

Language focus
use of the present perfect
simple with *just, already*
and *yet*

Pronunciation
weak form: *been* /bɪn/
linking: *just asked*

Preparation time
5 minutes

Game time
20 minutes

7.2

Record-breakers

Before class

Make one copy of the **Game board** (p.53) and one copy of each **Question sheet** (pp.54–5) for each group of four learners.

In class

1 This game is based on a board game where players try and build a path across a board while at the same time trying to block their opponents' path.

2 Explain that learners are going to play a game connected with world records. Put learners into pairs and seat them around the board as follows:

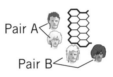

Give each pair one of the **Question sheets** (Pair A or Pair B) and tell them not to show or discuss it with the other pair.

3 The aim of the game is to be the first pair to form a continuous chain of hexagons from one side of the board to the other: Pair A (left to right); Pair B (top to bottom).

4 Pair A begins by choosing a subject from the hexagons on the board such as **CIRCUS**.

> Pair A: *We choose **CIRCUS**.*

Pair B then consults its **Question sheet** and reads out the corresponding question on the subject together with the three alternative answers:

> Pair B: *What's the longest anyone has ever spent on a tight-rope? Is it 4 days, 82 days or 259 days?*

If Pair A answers correctly first time, they can put a cross (X) on the CIRCUS hexagon. If Pair A answers incorrectly, Pair B should say that the answer is wrong, but not reveal the correct answer. It is now Pair B's turn to choose a hexagon and answer a question. Pair B should write a nought (O) on hexagons when they answer a question correctly.

Either pair can choose to answer a question on any hexagon on the board, either with the aim of forming a chain, or blocking the other pair.

Once an X or O is on a hexagon, the opposing pair is blocked from using this as part of their chain. As there are three answers, a pair can ask for the same question on a subsequent turn if they previously got it wrong.

Level
pre-intermediate – intermediate

Class size
groups of four

Language focus
present perfect simple (unspecified past time): *how many times / ever*

Pronunciation
weak forms: *been* /bɪn/ *has* /həz/ *have* /həv/

Preparation time
5 minutes

Game time
20 minutes

Game board

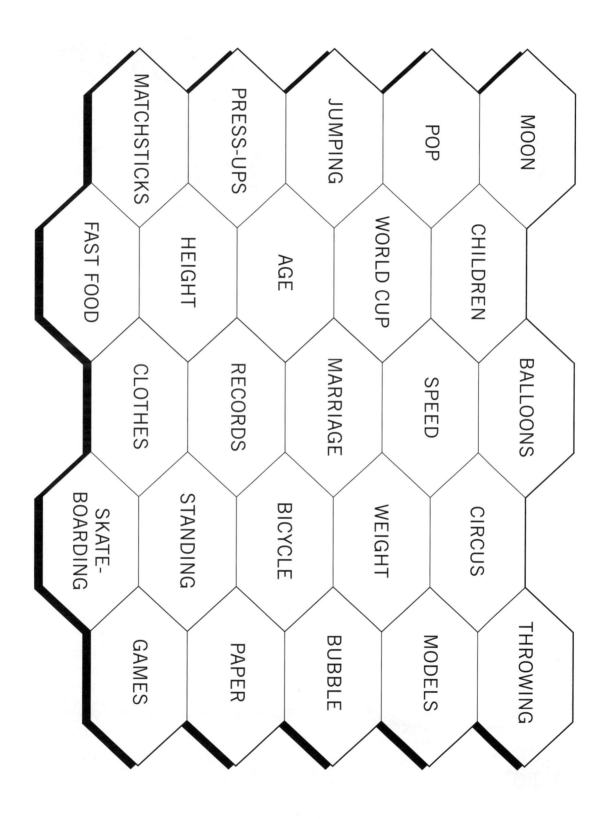

Pair A

Moon: How many times has a manned space flight landed on the moon? <u>6</u> 9 14

Pop: Which rock star has had the largest ever record contract? Madonna <u>Michael Jackson</u> Elvis

Jumping: What's the furthest distance anyone has ever jumped? 8.70 m <u>8.95 m</u> 9.21 m

Press-ups: What's the most press-ups anyone has ever done with one finger? <u>124</u> 128 466

Matchsticks: The largest object that has ever been made from matches is a: canoe <u>Rolls Royce</u> hang-glider

Children: What's the record number of times any woman has given birth? 24 <u>37</u> 42

World Cup: Which team has appeared in the World Cup finals the most times? <u>Brazil</u> Italy England

Age: What's the oldest age that any person has ever lived to? <u>122 years</u> 126 years 135 years

Height: The tallest that any man has ever been is: 2.55 m <u>2.72 m</u> 2.89 m

Throwing: The furthest anyone has ever thrown a playing card is: 18 m 49 m <u>61 m</u>

Models: The highest lego tower anyone has ever built is: 11.25 m <u>24.39 m</u> 56.47 m

Clothes: How long is the longest scarf anyone has ever made? 8 km <u>32 km</u> 85 km

Balloons: The largest number of people that have flown in a single air balloon flight is: 32 <u>50</u> 64

Speed: The fastest any boxer has knocked out an opponent is: 2 secs <u>20 secs</u> 64 secs

Marriage: The longest that any marriage has survived is: 75 years <u>86 years</u> 94 years

Records: Which singer has had the most singles in the US charts? <u>Elvis</u> Michael Jackson Diana Ross

Circus: What's the highest number of golf balls anyone has ever balanced on top of each other? <u>7</u> 10 16

Weight: The heaviest that any person has ever been is: <u>328 kg</u> 582 kg 635 kg

Fast food: What's the furthest distance anyone has thrown a hamburger from a pan? <u>25.5 m</u> 41 m 56 m

Bicycle: What's the fastest speed anyone has ever travelled on a bicycle? 69 mph 112 mph <u>152 mph</u>

Standing: What's the furthest anyone has ever crawled? 860 km <u>1,400 km</u> 4,600 km

Bubble: What's the diameter of the largest bubble-gum bubble anyone has ever blown? <u>58.4 cm</u> 83.6 cm 121.8 cm

Skateboarding: What's the highest anyone has jumped on a skateboard? 1.20 m <u>3.60 m</u> 2.02 m

Paper: The longest paper chain that has ever been made is: 36 km <u>59 km</u> 104 km

Games: The highest number of chess games anyone has ever played continuously is: 484 <u>633</u> 1,408

Records from *The Guinness Book of Records* 1990 edition © 1989 Guinness Publishing Ltd,
The Guinness Book of Records is a Trademark of Guinness Publishing Ltd.

Question sheet

Pair B

Moon: How many men have walked on the moon?
3 <u>12</u> 18

Pop: Which rock star/group has sold the most records? Elvis <u>The Beatles</u> Michael Jackson

Jumping: What's the greatest height anyone has ever jumped? 1.96 m 2.21 m <u>2.44 m</u>

Press-ups: What's the highest number of press-ups anyone has ever done within 24 hours?
328 650 <u>46,001</u>

Matchsticks: The furthest that anyone has flicked a match is: <u>34 m</u> 14 m 17 m

Children: What's the largest number of children any woman has had? 28 48 <u>69</u>

World Cup: Which team has scored the most goals in a World Cup? Brazil Germany <u>Hungary</u>

Age: The oldest age that any woman has ever lived to is: <u>118 years</u> 124 years 129 years

Height: The tallest any woman has ever been is: 2.25 m 2.37 m <u>2.48 m</u>

Bicycle: The furthest anyone has ever cycled in an hour is: 72.42 km <u>56.37 km</u> 104.06 km

Throwing: What's the furthest anyone has ever thrown a boomerang? <u>161 m</u> 242 m 368 m

Models: The height of the tallest snowman anyone has ever built is: 18.37 m <u>29.43 m</u> 35.64 m

Clothes: How old is the oldest piece of cloth that has ever been found?
2,700 years 6,400 years <u>9,000 years</u>

Balloons: What's the furthest distance a party balloon has ever travelled?
600 miles 2,800 miles <u>10,000 miles</u>

Speed: What's the fastest speed that any lift has ever travelled? <u>45 km/h</u> 65 km/h 110 km/h

Marriage: How many times has the most married man been married? 19 76 <u>28</u>

Records: Which artist has made the most records? Elvis <u>Mozart</u> The Beatles

Games: What's the longest time anyone has ever played computer games for?
46 hours <u>166 hours</u> 117 hours

Circus: What's the longest anyone has ever spent on a tight-rope? 4 days 82 days <u>259 days</u>

Weight: What's the greatest amount of weight anyone has lost on a diet? 69 kg <u>165 kg</u> 284 kg

Fast Food: What's the furthest distance anyone has travelled to get a take-away meal?
824 miles 3,255 miles <u>5,790 miles</u>

Standing: What's the longest time anyone has ever stood for? 18 days 244 days <u>17 years</u>

Skateboarding: What's the furthest anyone has ever jumped on a skateboard? <u>5.50 m</u> 6.40 m 7.20 m

Bubble: The length of the largest bubble anyone has ever blown is: <u>51 m</u> 22 m 29 m

Paper: The country which has had paper money the longest is: <u>China</u> India Britain

7.3

What have you done!

Before class
Make one copy of the **Exclamation cards** (p.57) for the whole group.

In class
1 This is a deduction game where teams race against each other to find an answer in response to a prompt.

2 Divide the class into roughly equal teams (approximately three to four teams). Depending on the size of the class, give each learner one or two cards but make sure that each team has roughly the same number of cards. Get learners to fold their cards along the line, so that when they hold up their exclamation, the present perfect sentence cannot be seen.

3 The aim of the game is to win as many **Exclamation cards** as possible by guessing the correct detail on the back of the card.

4 Nominate one team to start and ask one player in the team to hold up his/her exclamation and shout it out to the rest of the class. Players from the other teams now have to call out what they think has happened e.g.

> A: I'm full.
> B: You've had a problem?
> A: No.
> C: You've just had a meal.
> A: Yes. (Gives the card to the first team that guesses correctly.)

Only by giving one of the answers written on the back of the exclamation, can a team win a card.

5 The winning team is the one with most cards at the end of the game.

Level
pre-intermediate

Class size
whole class

Language focus
use of present perfect simple to talk about actions with present 'result'
use of mid-position adverb *just*

Pronunciation
weak form: *been* /bɪn/
linking: *just eaten* /jəs tiːtən/

Preparation time
5 minutes

Game time
20 minutes

Exclamation cards

I'm full. *you've just eaten/had a meal/dinner*	**Which channel?** *you've just turned on the TV*	**It's OK – I'll answer it!** *you've just heard the phone*
I look terrible there! *you've just seen a photograph*	**Wrong number, sorry.** *you've just answered the phone*	**That's odd, no-one's home.** *you've just rung the bell/knocked on the door*
And you are? *you've just introduced yourself/said your name*	**Yuk!** *you've just tasted something awful/terrible*	**I need a plaster/band-aid.** *you've just cut yourself*
Fasten your belt. *you've just got in a car*	**I need a sharpener.** *you've just broken your pencil*	**My feet are so wet.** *you've just been (out) in the rain*
Like my tan? *you've just been on holiday.*	**Which floor?** *you've just got in a lift*	**I need a rubber/an eraser.** *you've just made a mistake*
It fits. *you've just tried something on*	**I need a tissue now.** *you've just sneezed*	**There's no ice again.** *you've just opened the fridge/freezer*

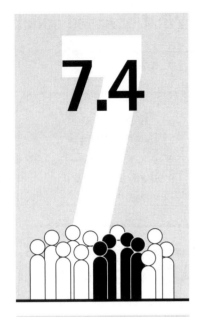

7.4 Jigsaw mischief

Level
intermediate –
upper-intermediate

Class size
groups of four

Language focus
present perfect
continuous: recent past
actions with visible present
effect

Pronunciation
fall–rise intonation in
questions; weak forms:
been /bɪn/ *you* /jə/

Preparation time
15 minutes

Game time
30 minutes

Before class

Make one complete set of the **Jigsaw pictures** (p.59) for every group of four learners. Cut each picture up along the jigsaw lines and keep the pieces of each picture together with a paper clip. Cut out the sentence strips and keep these with the appropriate jigsaw.

Give three jigsaws to one pair and three different jigsaws to the other pair they are playing against.

In class

1 This is a game where players take it in turns to slowly reveal the truth of a situation to other players. The latter must work out as quickly as possible what is happening.

2 Put learners into pairs and seat one pair with another pair against whom they are going to play. Explain to them that you are going to give them different jigsaws, which when complete show a teenager who has obviously been getting up to some kind of mischief.

3 The object of the game is to guess what mischief the character has been getting up to with as few jigsaw pieces as possible.

4 At the start of each round, give one pair in each group of four (Pair A) a jigsaw together with the appropriate sentence strip. Pair A should conceal the jigsaw and the sentence strip from Pair B.

Explain that Pair A start by laying down one jigsaw piece. Pair B now have one guess at what the character in the picture has been doing, e.g. *Have you been chasing a cat?* or one question that might help them to guess in a subsequent turn what the mischief is, e.g. *Have you been in someone's garden?*

Pair A answer *yes* or *no*. If the guess was incorrect, they then lay down another piece of the jigsaw. The players laying down the jigsaw pieces should obviously try to give away as little as possible each time. They can do this by putting down jigsaw pieces with the most peripheral information. They may also lay down non-adjacent pieces of the jigsaw.

5 At the end of each round, pairs should note down the number of pieces a pair were given before they guessed correctly. At the end of the six rounds, the pair with the lowest score are the winners.

Jigsaw pictures

You've been taking apples from the neighbour's garden.

You've been tying people's shoe laces together.

You've been copying from the person in front of you.

You've been putting chewing gum on other people's chairs.

You've been pressing the stop button on the bus.

You've been playing your music too loudly.

7.5

Adverb rummy

Before class
Make one copy of the **Rummy cards** (p.61) for each group of three learners.

In class
1 This is a card game similar to a game played with a real pack of cards where players have a hand and take it in turns to pick up and throw away cards.

2 Each group plays with one set of cards. Explain that there are 'sentence' cards (white) and 'time adverb' cards (shaded). Ask one player to shuffle the cards and deal seven cards to him/herself and seven to the other two players. Put the remaining cards face-down in a pile, except for the top one which is turned up next to the pile.

3 The aim of the game is to get 'rummy':

> two 'sentence' cards that go with one 'time adverb' card
> three 'sentence' cards that go with another 'time adverb' card

Example:

I've not been feeling well at all	She's been getting better marks	**lately**
Someone stole my bike	My sister started college	My team lost badly	**last week**

4 Players take it in turns to pick up a card: either one from the top of the pack, or the one showing, i.e. the card the last player threw away. After deciding whether to keep the card, the player then throws one away.

5 When a player thinks he/she has 'rummy', he/she should put down his/her cards. If the other players agree, the group can reshuffle the cards and begin a new game. If they do not agree – you can act as judge – the player picks his/her cards up again and the game continues. The player that wins the most games is the winner.

The game can be used to practise the contrast between the present perfect simple and simple past only, or the cards above the thick dotted line can be added for further contrast with the present perfect continuous.

Level
intermediate –
upper-intermediate

Class size
groups of three

Language focus
contrast present perfect
simple/continuous and
simple past

Pronunciation
weak forms: *been* /bɪn/
to /tə/

Preparation time
10 minutes

Game time
20 minutes

Rummy cards

I've been doing my homework	Our teacher has been working at the school	My brother has been collecting stamps
She's been getting better marks	I've been playing for the first team	I've not been feeling well at all

present perfect continuous

all day	over the past few weeks	since last year	lately

I didn't have anything to eat	I went camping with my parents	Someone stole my bike	My team lost badly
Who saw the programme on TV	Our neighbours bought a pet snake	My sister started college	Dear Pete, I was pleased to receive your letter

simple past

during the summer	at the weekend	earlier	last week

It's been a lot of fun	I've been on a plane	We've already changed teachers	I have never sat an exam like this
There have been a lot of students in the library	I haven't seen her new film	How many goals have they scored	Have you started your dancing classes
Our trip has been cancelled	Who have you invited	We haven't used the computers	Our country has bid to hold the Olympics

present perfect simple

several times	before	so far	recently
yet	this week		

From **The Grammar Activity Book** by Bob Obee © Cambridge University Press 1999 **PHOTOCOPIABLE**

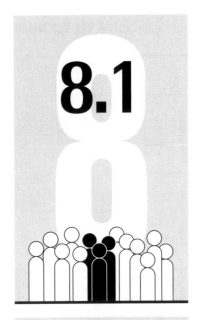

8.1

Determiner dominoes

Before class
Copy and cut out one set of **Domino pieces** *(see below) (p.63) for each group of three learners.

In class
1 Explain to learners that they are going to play a game of dominoes. Draw some domino pieces on the board and elicit from learners how the real game of dominoes is played. Make sure that all learners understand the principle of the game.

2 Give each group of three learners a set of dominoes and ask one player to deal ten pieces to each person in the group. Tell learners they should spread their pieces out so that they can see them all, but also that they should conceal their pieces from the other players.

3 One player starts the game by putting a piece in the middle. The next player then puts down a piece to make a grammatically correct determiner/noun combination and so on!

4 If a player thinks he/she cannot go, the next player simply takes the turn. If a player puts down a piece that any of the other players feel makes an incorrect combination, the grammar point should be discussed. If players cannot agree, they should call the teacher to act as judge. If it is found to be wrong, the player takes the piece back and misses the turn.

5 The winner of the game is the first player to have played all his/her pieces, or the player with the fewest pieces when no more pieces can be laid down.

*Use the first 18 pieces plus the 12 black pieces for pre-intermediate level and the same 12 black pieces plus the last 16 pieces for upper-intermediate level.

Level
pre-intermediate –
upper-intermediate

Class size
groups of three

Language focus
use of determiners with
singular, plural and
uncountable nouns.

Pronunciation
weak form: *some* /səm/

Preparation time
10 minutes

Game time
25 minutes

Domino pieces

furniture	not much
bread	not many
newspaper	enough
people	every
bicycle	each
women	another
money	both
trouble	not many
mice	a/an
soap	each
equipment	a few
environment	little
cattle	less
information	a few
trip	less

sheep	some
price	a/an
homework	all
sports	too much
cartoons	too many
matches	a/an
friends	not much
laughter	a/an
notebook	all
news	another
trousers	other
crowd	neither
friendship	either
leather	several
problems	other
computers	fewer

holidays	each
game	enough
suitcases	some
chocolate	both
letters	another
dollar	all
sleep	some
address	enough
CD	too many
luggage	some
luck	several
series	whole
toys	few
advice	either
heroes	little

8.2

Pieces of me

Level
intermediate –
upper-intermediate

Class size
whole class

Language focus
partitive nouns e.g. *slice*
and collective nouns
e.g. *flock*

Pronunciation
weak form: *of* /əv/

Preparation time
5 minutes

Game time
25 minutes

Before class

Make one copy of the **Noun cards** (p.65) for the whole class. Bring some sticky tape or safety pins to class for learners to attach the cards to their clothing. You will also need something to stick the words to the board.

In class

1 This is a 'mingle' activity where learners race to find a grammatical 'partner'.

2 Put learners into pairs (or groups of three if a large class) and divide the **Noun cards** equally among the pairs. Provide each pair with some means of sticking/tacking a card to their clothing. Arrange the class so that there is some space for about half the members to mingle.

Version 1

1 The aim of the game is to be the first pair to find grammatical partners for all the words on the cards the pair is given at the start of the game.

2 Each pair should have a 'home' desk where the cards should be placed. When pairs have been given the cards, ask them to write one of their names (small) in the corner of the card. Ask one player from each pair to pin/stick a card to his clothing and mingle with the players from the other pairs to find a compatible noun.

When two learners have found a match, they should run to the board and tell you the phrase, for example: *a bar of soap/a slice of bread*

If it is correct, put the cards on the board; if not, send them away.

Players return to their 'home' either when they have found a successful match or when they decide there is no suitable matching item in the mingle of learners. The other member of the pair then sticks/pins on another Noun card and mingles.

3 The winner is the first pair to have all its Noun cards stuck on the board. Use the names on the cards to get learners to tell the class about their noun phrases.

Version 2

1 This version of the game is more difficult, so should be played with learners of a higher level. Remove all the partitive noun cards from **Version 1**, e.g. *piece*, *bar*, *slice* etc., and add the other uncountable and plural **Noun cards** marked **Version 2**.

2 Although the procedure for playing the game is identical to Version 1, this time players have to find a partner noun that can be quantified in the same way. For example, learners run to the board and say:

'We are both bunches!'   *'We are both pieces!'*

3 To make this version easier, write some or all of the partitive nouns that learners will be looking for around the edge of the board, *e.g: bunch round piece pack*

4 As before, the winner of the game is the first pair to have all its **Noun cards** stuck to the board.

Noun cards

Version 1

slice	slice	bar
bar	pair	pair
pair	tube	packet
packet	block	lump
crowd	pack	

soap	chocolate	bread
meat	trousers	gloves
glasses	biscuits	cigarettes
flats	sugar	people
cards	toothpaste	

Version 2

ice	keys	flowers
equipment	luggage	information
advice	binoculars	birds
applause	golf	coal
demonstrators	wolves	friends
tourists	glue	sheep

Partitive/collective common denominators for Version 2
pair slice round flock lump block piece pack
crowd group tube packet bar bunch

8.3 Building captions

Level
intermediate

Class size
groups of three

Language focus
use of *the*/zero article with singular/plural/uncountable nouns

Pronunciation
the /ðə/ *the* /ði:/ before vowels and consonants

Preparation time
5 minutes

Game time
25 minutes

Before class

Make one copy of the **Cartoon sheet** (p.67) for each group of three learners. You may wish to write the **Building blocks** below on a poster or OHT to save time in class.

In class

1 This activity is a puzzle-solving exercise where learners are given the words from seven original cartoon captions and they have to sort them out.

2 Write the following **Building blocks** on the board or use an OHT prepared earlier.

Articles	Nouns	Other words	
0	children	new	They're
0	Italian	it's	He's
0	goalkeeper	not	Okay
the	Parrots	I hate	bite
0	endings	Do you	or
the	Chinese	sad	related to
the	Apes	fancy	great
the	footprints	They'd make	I'm
0	sleeping bags	He's	wonderful with
0			

3 Put learners into groups of three and give each one a **Cartoon sheet**. Explain that what they have to do is build the original short captions of each cartoon. All of the words they need are in the building blocks and for each caption they need to use at least one word from each block. (The zero article (0) has been listed for each time it needs to be used.)

An additional element you can introduce into the game is to allow each team three questions. One group member should come up to you and ask the question and then go back and give the answer to his/her group. For example:

Does the lion ask: 'Do you fancy something?'

4 The winner of the game is the first group to get all the original captions sorted out using all of the words in the building blocks.

Captions:	Cartoons:
He's wonderful with children ...	a
Parrots bite.	e
He's the new goalkeeper.	g
Do you fancy the Chinese or the Italian?	d
I hate sad endings.	f
They'd make great sleeping bags.	b
They're not footprints.	c
I'm related to the Apes.	h

Cartoon sheet

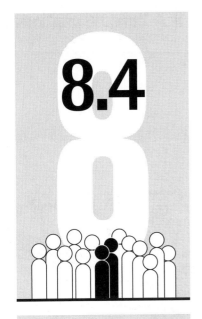

8.4

Open 'the' doors

Level
intermediate –
upper-intermediate

Class size
pairs

Language focus
use of zero article with
certain classes of noun:
*institutions, means of
transport, times of day,
seasons, meals, illnesses.*

Pronunciation
the /ðə/ *the* /ði:/ before
vowels and consonants;
weak form: *at* /ət/

Preparation time
5 minutes

Game time
10–15 minutes

Before class
Make one copy of the **Maze** (p.69) for each pair of students.

In class
1 This is an activity where learners are placed in the centre of a maze.
As with a real maze, there are some doors they can pass through to get out,
and others that will not help them to escape.

2 Divide learners into pairs. Distribute one copy of the **Maze** to each pair.
Explain that you are going to put them in a maze (they start in the middle)
and what they have to do is to find their way out as quickly as possible.
To get out they can only go through doors where they have to put 'the' for the
phrase to be grammatically correct.

All those doors (phrases) where the zero article is either acceptable or usual
are locked and entrance is not allowed.

3 The aim is to be the first pair to have found a route out.

4 Make it clear to the class that they have to find a complete route out before
you will check their answers. Tell them there is only one correct way out. (See
Key below). When one pair have found a route out they should shout '*Out*'. One
member of the pair should then read out their route to the rest of the class:

   in the library ...   in the south ... etc.

As soon as the pair makes a mistake say: '*Blocked!*' and ask everyone to
continue the search. You might also like to encourage members of the class to
shout out *blocked* if they feel a pair has made a mistake. The 'blocked' pair can
only have a turn at reading out a route again after another pair has had a turn.

5 The first pair to find a correct route out are the winners.

> **Key:**
> in the post → on the radio → in the daytime → at the end →
> on the stairs → on the phone → in the past

As a follow-up, you could ask learners to look back at the maze and find the
six types of noun that are often used with the zero article, see below.

> Times of day and night ... especially after *at by after* and ***before***
>
> Meals ... when talked about as part of the day
>
> Seasons ... when talked about generally
>
> Illnesses ...
>
> Means of transport ... after ***by***
>
> Certain places ... when talked about as 'institutions' rather than specific
> 'places/buildings'

Maze

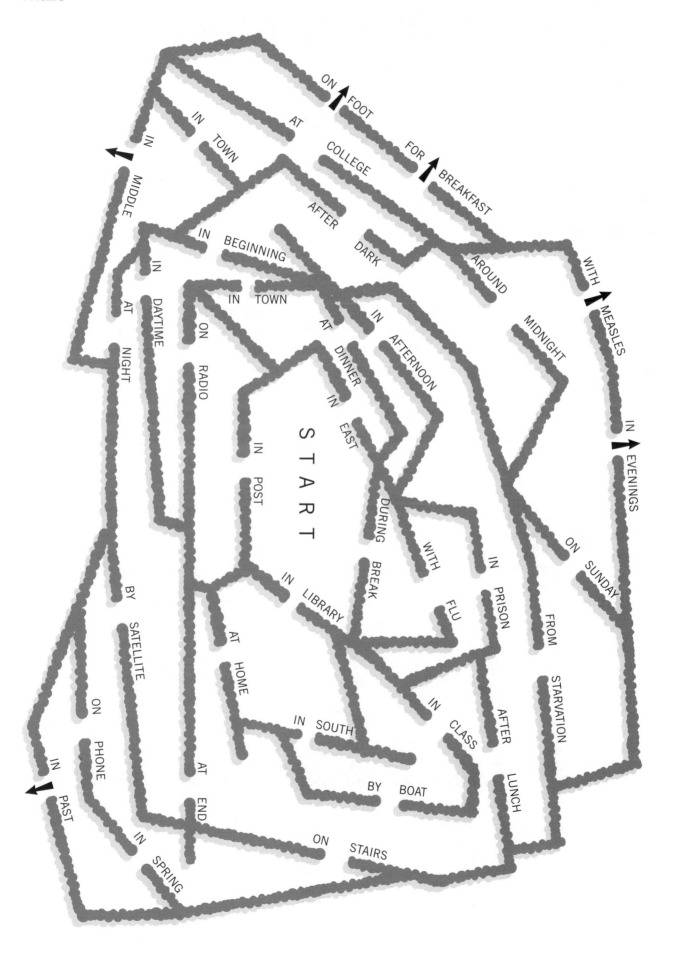

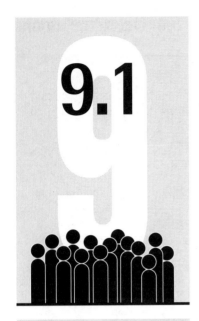

9.1

Homophone healing

Before class
Make one copy of the four sets of **Homophone cards** (p.71) for teams A–D.
Cut up each set of cards so that you have six cards for each team.

In class
1 This is a game where learners write riddles for other members of the class to solve.

2 Divide the class into four teams (A, B, C and D). Explain what a homophone is and give each team one set of six homophones and ask learners to spread them out on a desk in front of them. Explain to learners that what they have to do is to write a sentence saying how you have to change the word on the left-hand side of the card to make it become the word on the right-hand side of the card (homophone).

Example: **NO → KNOW**

If you add a first and last letter, you get a clever verb.

3 The aim of the game is to solve the other teams' riddles as quickly as possible.

4 Ask players to work in their teams to write riddles for all the homophones they have. When all teams have done this, you are ready to begin the game.

Explain to learners that the game will be played in two separate rounds; in one round they will provide the clues, in the other round they will have to solve them.

Write in large letters on the board the words on the left-hand side of the 12 homophone cards that were given to Teams A and B. In this round Teams C and D compete against each other. You may alternatively wish to put these words on an OHT before class.

Ask a member from Teams A and B to read out one (any) of their sentences. In response to the riddle, members of Teams C and D scan the board and try and be the first team to shout out the correct answer. Repeat this process for all the words on the board, asking a different player to read out a riddle each time and score one point for each word a team gets.

Reverse the process so that the words from Teams C and D go up on the board and Teams A and B now compete against each other.

With more able classes you might choose to adapt the guessing stage, for example giving them the clues (not the first word).

5 The winner of the game is the team that scored the most points overall. Keep scores on the board.

Level
intermediate

Class size
whole class

Language focus
use of zero conditional to talk about general truths

Pronunciation
third person ending: /s/ /z/ /iz/

Preparation time
5 minutes

Game time
30 minutes

Homophone cards ✂

Team A

flower → flour	red → read
poor → pour	fair → fare
stalk → stork	roll → role

Team B

stair → stare	night → knight
week → weak	dear → deer
piece → peace	mail → male

Team C

right → write	pear → pair
wait → weight	sure → shore
bear → bare	guest → guessed

Team D

hole → whole	break → brake
blue → blew	allowed → aloud
board → bored	heard → herd

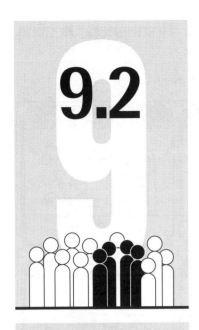

9.2

Blanks and brackets

Before class

Make copies of **Sheet 1** for half the class and copies of **Sheet 2** (both p.73) for the other half of the class. Make sure that you keep **Sheets 1** and **2** separate as it is important that pairs playing against each other do not see the other pair's sheet.

In class

1 This is a game of speculation where players race to complete a grid.

2 Divide the class into pairs. Arrange the class so that each pair sits facing its opponents. Distribute Sheets 1 and 2 to opposing pairs. Ensure that learners understand that they must keep their sheet hidden from the opposition.

3 Explain that the aim of the game is to complete the blank grid by finding the responses that were made to the simple statements. Tell students that all the responses are built around one of the following words: *if*, *unless* or *in case*. For example, one line of one grid might look like this:

		A	B	C	D	E	F	G
I'm hungry	1	[ ]	[ ]	_____	[ ]	_____	_____	_____

The response players will have to find for these squares is:

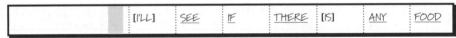

	[I'LL]	SEE	IF	THERE	[IS]	ANY	FOOD

Each pair is attempting to complete its own grid while at the same holding the completed key to its opponent's grid.

4 Explain to learners that each pair takes it in turns to try to find something that goes in one of the spaces on their grid. There are two ways to do this:

For the blanks: Players with **Sheet 1**, for example, might say the word *we* and the players with **Sheet 2** now have to reveal whether that word belongs on any of the blanks on the grid.

They either answer *no* or give the coordinates for one instance of where the word occurs on a blank. For example,

Is the word 'we' on the grid?
Yes. It's A3.

Any space marked with a line represents one word.

The pair with **Sheet 1** can now fill this in on their grid. And it is now the turn of the pair with **Sheet 2** to ask a question.

For the brackets [ ] – which could be one or two words – players have to ask directly. For example:

Is B1 'I'll'?

The other pair respond *yes* or *no*.

5 The game continues with pairs taking it in turns to guess in one of these two ways until one pair has completed its grid. The first pair to do so is the winner.

Level
intermediate

Class size
groups of four

Language focus
first conditional: use of *if, unless, in, case*

Pronunciation
contraction: *won't* /wəunt/ *unless* /ənles/

Preparation time
5 minutes

Game time
20 minutes

9.2 Blanks and brackets

Sheet 1

Sheet 1		A	B	C	D	E	F	G
'I might not be in.'	1	[ ]	____	____	____	[ ]	[ ]	____
'It starts at 8.00.'	2	[ ]	____	____ ,	[ ]	____	____ .	
'Our captain is ill.'	3	____	[ ]	____			[ ]	____
'It's very cloudy.'	4	[ ]	____			[ ]	____	[ ]
'I'm not going.'	5	____	[ ]	____			[ ] .	

		A	B	C	D	E	F	G
'I need to see Jim.'	1	IF	I	[SEE]	HIM,	[I'LL]	TELL	HIM
'It might be cold.'	2	[I'LL]	BRING	A	COAT	[IN CASE]	IT	[IS]
'I've got exams soon.'	3	[YOU'LL]	PASS	[IF]	YOU	[STUDY]	HARD.	
'My leg still hurts.'	4	IT	[WON'T]	GET	BETTER	[UNLESS]	YOU	[REST]
'They could arrive early.'	5	[I'LL]	STAY	HOME	[IN CASE]	THEY	DO	

✂ -

Sheet 2

Sheet 2		A	B	C	D	E	F	G
'I need to see Jim.'	1	____	____	[ ]	____ .	[ ]	____	____
'It might be cold.'	2	[ ]	____	____		[ ]	____	[ ]
'I've got exams soon.'	3	[ ]	____	[ ]	____	[ ]	____ .	
'My leg still hurts.'	4	____	[ ]	____		[ ]	____	[ ]
'They could arrive early.'	5	[ ]	____	____	[ ]	____	[ ] .	

		A	B	C	D	E	F	G
'I might not be in.'	1	[I'LL]	LEAVE	A	MESSAGE	[IF]	[YOU'RE]	OUT
'It starts at 8.00.'	2	[WE'LL]	BE	LATE	[UNLESS]	WE	HURRY	
'Our captain is ill.'	3	WE	[WON'T]	WIN	IF	HE	[DOESN'T]	PLAY
'It's very cloudy.'	4	[I'LL]	TAKE	AN	UMBRELLA	[IN CASE]	IT	[RAINS]
'I'm not going.'	5	I	[WON'T]	GO	UNLESS	YOU	[DO].	

9.3

Seeking scruples

Level
intermediate

Class size
groups of three

Language focus
second conditional:
If I found a wounded bird, I'd …

Pronunciation
contractions: *I'd* /aɪd/
wouldn't /wʊdnt/

Preparation time
5 minutes

Game time
35 minutes

Before class

Make enough copies of the **Scruples sheets** (p.75) to give each group of three learners one copy of one sheet 'sheet 1' or 'sheet 2'. Do not give every group the same sheet. Also give each group three cards, one with **A** written on it, another with **B** written on it and a third with **C** written on it. The letters on these cards should be clearly visible to the whole class when held up.

In class

1 This is a game where players have to predict how other players would behave in certain situations. It works best with classes that know each other well.

2 Divide the class into groups of three (two if you have a small class) and give each group a **Scruples sheet**. Explain the idea of scruples (moral behaviour) to the class. You might like to illustrate with the following example: you are in a fast food shop and the assistant gives you a much bigger order than you've paid for, what would you do? Elicit from players what the various courses of action might be.

3 The aim of the game is to be the group that most correctly predicts how other players would behave in situations where their morals are tested.

4 Ask players to complete their **Scruples sheet** – completing both questions and answers – so that they can put the 'scruples' questions to other members of the class. Point out to learners that each question involves a three-option multiple-choice answer: **A**, **B** or **C**.

When groups have completed their **Scruples sheets**, you are ready to begin the game. Place a chair at the front of the class and call out one player to sit on it for each round. Nominate another player to ask this player a particular question and ask the player to write down his/her answer: **A**, **B** or **C** (i.e. what he/she would do in this particular situation). When he/she has written the answer, ask every group (apart from the player's own team) to hold up the letter that they think will correspond to the player's answer. The player in the chair then reveals his/her answer, i.e. only after members from other groups have shown what they think he/she will answer. Repeat the process with a different player and question each time.

5 Keep group scores. Score one point for each answer correctly predicted. The first group to reach six points are the winners.

Note: It does not matter if a question is used more than once as long as it is asked to a different person.

Scruples sheets

Sheet 1

◆ If a fly was annoying you in your room, would you:
  a kill it with your hand
  b spray it
  c _____

◆ _____
  _____
  a take it to the police station
  b keep it
  c _____

◆ If you saw someone break a school window, would you:
  a tell a teacher
  b _____
  c _____

◆ If you were sitting on a crowded bus and several old people were standing,
  _____ :
  a get up as if you were getting off
  b _____
  c _____

◆ If you found a love letter addressed to a friend, would you:
  a put it on a notice-board
  b _____
  c _____

◆ _____
  _____
  a tell the shop assistant his mistake
  b not say anything and spend it
  c wait until you were outside to decide

◆ If you were suddenly caught chewing bubble gum when you shouldn't be,
  _____:
  a stick it under some furniture
  b _____
  c try and save it for later

◆ If you _____
  _____
  a _____
  b _____
  c _____

Sheet 2

◆ If something was incorrectly priced (much too cheaply) in a supermarket, would you:
  a check if there was a mistake
  b try and buy as many as you could
  c _____

◆ _____
  _____
  a just say it was an accident
  b try and fix it and say nothing
  c offer to pay for a new one

◆ If you were standing in a queue and someone older came and stood in front of you, would you:
  a say nothing
  b _____
  c jump in front of them when it's your turn

◆ If you felt ill just before your team had a big game, would you:
  a say you shouldn't play
  b _____
  c _____

◆ If you thought someone was wearing a wig.
  _____ :
  a _____
  b _____
  c keep talking about hair

◆ If you bought two ice-creams and one was much bigger than the other,
  _____ :
  a give your friend the smaller one
  b ask your friend which one he wanted
  c _____

◆ If in a cinema a couple in front of you were kissing during a film, would you:
  a move seats
  b _____
  c _____

◆ If you _____
  _____
  _____
  a _____
  b _____
  c _____

9.4

Memory consequences

Before class

Make one copy of the **Consequences sheet** (p.77) for each member of the class. Make one copy of the **Picture sheet** (also p.77). Either put this on an overhead transparency or enlarge it so that the pictures can be seen by all members of the class when held up at the front of the class.

In class

1 This game is a memory competition where learners have to make associations between images they see and clues in front of them.

2 Divide the class into groups of three or four and give everyone a **Consequences sheet**. Explain that groups can win points by making connections between the half sentences in front of them and remembering things they have been shown.

3 The aim of the game is for groups to complete as many of the sentences as possible, in a race against other groups.

4 Tell learners that at the beginning of each round you will show a sheet of pictures for about two or three seconds to the whole class. They then have to make a connection between one of the pictures they can remember and the half sentences in front of them and complete the sentence appropriately (hypothetical consequence + past action). For example,

We would have won [picture of ball missing basketball shot] *if he/she hadn't missed the shot.*

As soon as learners think they have an answer, they should shout it out. If it is correct, their group wins the sentence. Show the pictures again when you think learners are unlikely to make any more connections.

5 The group with the most sentences wins the game. As the game progresses, groups should be able to remember more and more of the pictures each time they are shown and may, therefore, give you more than one correct sentence each time.

For weaker classes you might consider showing the pictures for a longer period each time.

Level
intermediate – upper-intermediate

Class size
whole class

Language focus
third conditional: *If you hadn't done ...,*

Pronunciation
would have /wʊdəv/
wouldn't have /wʊdənəv/

Preparation time
5 minutes

Game time
20 minutes

Key:

We would have won	**if he/she hadn't missed the shot (11)**
We would have gone swimming	**if it had been warmer (2)**
The fire wouldn't have started	**if you hadn't left the iron on (6)**
The dog wouldn't have got out	**if you hadn't left the gate open (12)**
I would have believed you	**if it hadn't been April Fool's Day (10)**
You wouldn't have burnt	**if you had put sun cream on (3)**
You wouldn't have caught a cold	**if you had put your coat on (7)**
The thief wouldn't have got in	**if you hadn't left the window open (4)**
It would have tasted better	**if you had added salt (8)**
The neighbours wouldn't have complained	**if you hadn't played your hi-fi so loudly (13)**
The plant wouldn't have died	**if you had watered it (4)**
I would have rung	**if I had had a phone card (1)**
He wouldn't have been caught	**if he hadn't left his fingerprint (5)**
I would have been here sooner	**If I hadn't had a flat tyre (9)**

Consequences sheet

We would have won
We would have gone swimming
The fire wouldn't have started
The dog wouldn't have got out
I would have believed you
You wouldn't have burnt
You wouldn't have caught a cold

The thief wouldn't have got in
It would have tasted better
The neighbours wouldn't have complained
The plant wouldn't have died
I would have rung
He wouldn't have been caught
I would have been here sooner

Picture sheet

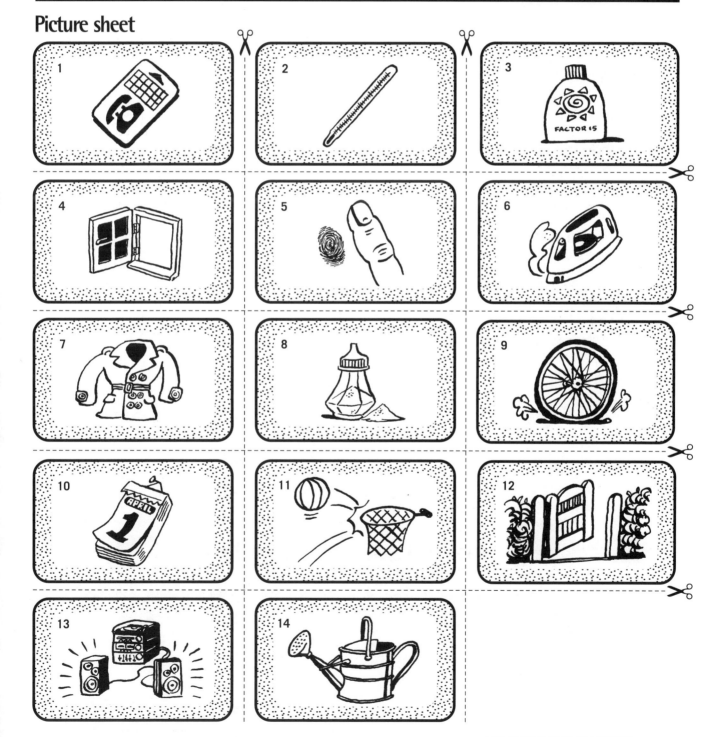

From **The Grammar Activity Book** by Bob Obee © Cambridge University Press 1999 **PHOTOCOPIABLE** 77

10.1 Headline investment

Before class

Make one copy of the **Headline sheet** (p.79) for each group of three learners and one copy of the **Newspaper story summaries** (also p.79) so that you can give details of the story at the appropriate point. This activity can obviously be adapted to work with other texts done in class.

In class

1 Explain to learners the idea of 'odds' which are based on how likely/unlikely something is to happen. For example, if it only snows at Christmas about once every five years, we might say: the odds of it snowing at Christmas are about 5/1. In this game, however, 'odds' refer to how easy or difficult it is to see a connection between two things.

2 Explain to learners that you are going to give them a list of headlines about unusual stories and also a number of words from the stories that the headlines relate to, with odds next to them: 3/1, 8/1 etc. Divide the class into groups of three. Tell learners that each group will be given £80 which they have to invest by making eight choices (8 × £10) as to which words appeared in which story.

In their groups learners first try and deduce which words go with which headlines, and then write their choices in the column next to the headlines e.g.

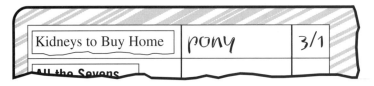

Explain to the class that they can choose more than one word for each headline.

3 The aim of the game is to invest the money as wisely as possible and get as much back as you can.

4 When learners have made their choices, write the first headline on the board and ask each group if they chose any words for that headline. Ask one or two groups to explain what they think the connection might be between the headline and the word(s) they have chosen. Then reveal which words go with the story by reading the story summary.

Any group that gets a word from the story correct wins whatever the odds were, multiplied by the £10 investment e.g. 3/1 × 10 = £30

5 Repeat this process for each headline. The group that has made the most money at the end of the game wins the game.

Level
intermediate

Class size
groups of three

Language focus
speculation and deduction (*could, might, might not, can't, must*)

Pronunciation
weak form: *must* /məs(t)/

Preparation time
5 minutes

Game time
25 minutes

Headline sheet

Investments

Headline			Keyword		Odds	Keyword		Odds
Kidneys to Buy Home			rainstorm		evens	distance		6/1
All the Sevens			month		2/1	English		6/1
The Penalty War			teams		2/1	2,000 people		8/1
A Living Toy			pony		3/1	extra		8/1
The Frog Shower			orphans		3/1	Central American		12/1
Sewing by Puppy Power			farmer		4/1			
Total money made:			wheels		4/1			

Newspaper story summaries

Kidneys to Buy Home
A 21-year-old Brazilian girl with two **extra** kidneys is hoping to sell them to buy a house for her five **orphaned** brothers. The girl, Odete Lopes, hopes to sell them for about £16,000 each.

The Frog Shower
A shower of frogs which darkened the air and covered the ground for a long **distance** is reported to be the result of a recent **rainstorm** in Kansas City, Mo.

All the Sevens
On the seventh day of the seventh month (7th July 1977), a certain Mrs Severn became 77.

The Penalty War
In June 1969, the **Central American** football **teams** of Honduras and El Salvador played a series of qualifying matches for the World Cup. The games were closely fought, and El Salvador eventually won after being awarded a disputed penalty. Rioting broke out at the ground, and the fighting spilled into the streets. In July, war was declared between the two countries as a direct result of the disputed penalty. **Two thousand people** died in the fighting.

Sewing by Puppy Power
Among the forgotten marvels of Victorian invention, one device caused considerable outcry during the 1870s. This was the dog-driven sewing machine. The apparatus was marketed and actually used in some **English** households, employing a special set of **wheels** which were moved by a little dog on a leash.

A Living Toy
An 18-inch Shetland **pony** has been bred by Mr Ray Allman, a **farmer** of Madley Heath, North Staffordshire.

10.2

Streetwise surveys

Level
pre-intermediate – intermediate

Class size
whole class

Language focus
use of *must, mustn't, have to, don't have to*

Pronunciation
weak forms: *must* /məs(t)/ *have* /həv/ *to* /tə/

Preparation time
5 minutes

Game time
30 minutes

Before class
For this game, the class should be divided into four roughly equal teams, **A–D**. Each team is to be given one of the **Survey sheets** (p.81) and you will need to make one copy for every member of the team.

In class
1 This is an activity where learners have to survey the opinions of as many learners from other groups (or people outside the class) as they can and use the results in a game of speculation.

2 Divide the class into four teams and give each team a different **Survey sheet**. Ask learners to discuss in their teams how they are going to ask the questions in their survey. For example,

something/not/drink/eat/before bed
Name something that you mustn't eat or drink before you go to bed.

Go around helping and checking at this stage to make sure learners are producing the language correctly.

Now ask learners to mingle in class or to interview people outside the class. If surveying in class, learners find a member of another team, ask one question and note down his/her answer. They then let the other learners ask them one question and then move on to another learner. If a learner has already been asked a question, he/she should say *'I've been asked that'*, and allow another question. Allow about 15 minutes for this.

Learners then return to their teams and compile the results of their survey. Ask one member of each team to act as secretary.

What learners need to do is to work out what the top two answers for each of the questions they asked were. For example:

Name something you mustn't eat or drink before you go to bed.

If, from the survey, four people said *coffee*, two *chocolate*, one *tea*, one *cheese* then the top two answers were 'coffee' and 'chocolate'.

When teams have worked out their survey answers, you are ready to begin the scoring stage of the game.

3 The aim of the game now is to guess what the majority of people who were surveyed said in response to each question.

4 Team A begins by asking one member of Team B a question like this:

We said: *Name something that you mustn't eat or drink before you go to bed. What were the top two answers?*

If that person can present two correct answers, he/she scores a point for Team B. If not, Teams C and D may offer answers. The first member from one of the two other teams to shout out the correct answer wins the point.

5 Team A now asks the next question to a member of a different team, e.g. Team C or D. The team with the most points at the end of the game wins.

Survey sheet

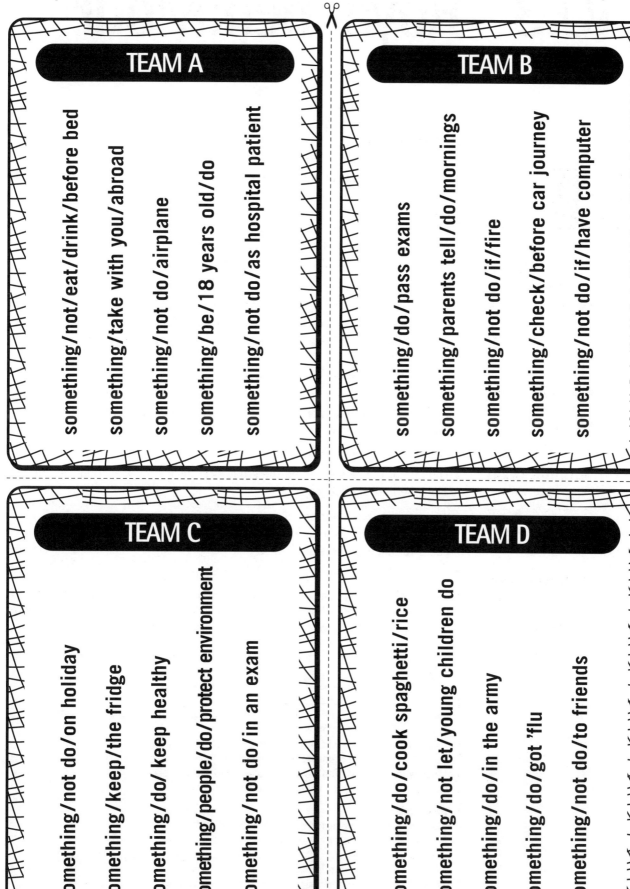

TEAM A

something/not/eat/drink/before bed

something/take with you/abroad

something/not do/airplane

something/be/18 years old/do

something/not do/as hospital patient

TEAM B

something/do/pass exams

something/parents tell/do/mornings

something/not do/if/fire

something/check/before car journey

something/not do/if/have computer

TEAM C

something/not do/on holiday

something/keep/the fridge

something/do/ keep healthy

something/people/do/protect environment

something/not do/in an exam

TEAM D

something/do/cook spaghetti/rice

something/not let/young children do

something/do/in the army

something/do/got 'flu

something/not do/to friends

10.3

unit 10 Obligation and possibility

Royal behaviour

Level
intermediate –
upper-intermediate

Class size
groups of three or four

Language focus
modals speculation about
past: *must have/might
have/couldn't have*

Pronunciation
must have /məstəv/
could have /kʊdəv/
couldn't have /kʊdənəv/
been /bɪn/

Preparation time
5 minutes

Game time
20 minutes

Before class
Make one copy of the **Royal behaviour sheet** (p.83) for every group of three members of the class or one copy on an OHT to show the whole class.

In class
1 Tell learners that they are going to play a game where they will have to speculate about unusual behaviour and events. All the statements they will be presented with are about rulers of the past.

2 Divide the class into groups of three learners. Learners have to discuss each statement and speculate on the reasons for it. They should then write down their speculations. (Allow about ten minutes for this.) If learners are confident about their speculations, they may express themselves using *must have/couldn't have/can't have* e.g.

He must have suffered from headaches.

If learners are less confident about their speculations, and only want to offer a 'suggestion', they may express themselves using *could have/might have/might not have* e.g.

He might have suffered from headaches.

3 The aim of the game is to be the group that most accurately deduces the reasons behind the actions.

4 When groups have written all their answers, ask them to read out their speculations about the first statement. Note down the scores. Repeat the process for each of the statements.

5 Scoring: 3 points when learners have correctly speculated about an event. However, they lose 1 point for incorrect speculation. 1 point when learners offer correctly expressed suggestion. If the suggestion is incorrect, learners do not lose a point. The group with the most points at the end wins.

Key:	
King Pepi:	This was in order to keep the flies away.
King John:	He suffered from sea-sickness.
James:	They forgot to paint him/wanted to paint him after his death.
Louis:	He hated washing.
Victoria:	She was afraid of dropping the children.
Luis:	He died/was killed in battle.
Ferdinand:	He didn't want his picture to be stamped.
George:	He was always afraid of being late.
Extension:	
Catherine:	She discovered she had dandruff.
Juana:	She promised they would never be apart.
Ludwig II:	He did it for good luck – he believed a peasant a day kept the doctors away.
Edward VI:	No-one was allowed to smack the king.
Philippe:	His mother wanted to have a girl.
Shih Huang Ti:	He was afraid of assassination.
Mithridates:	He wanted to be immune in case someone tried to poison him.
Jan Zizka:	He wanted it to be played in future battles.

Royal behaviour sheet

◆ King Pepi II of ancient Egypt always kept slaves around him who were covered in honey.

◆ King John (reigned 1199–1216) employed someone to hold his head (the royal head holder) whenever he went to sea.

◆ James, Duke of Monmouth (1649–1685), who was beheaded after he tried to become king, had his head sewn back on after his death.

◆ Louis XIV of France (reigned 1643–1715) only took three baths in the whole of his adult life.

◆ In her later years, whenever Queen Victoria (reigned 1837–1901) posed for a photograph holding one of her grandchildren, one of her servants hid beneath her skirt.

◆ Crown Prince Luis Filipe of Portugal was king of Portugal for about 20 minutes.

◆ King Ferdinand of Sicily (reigned 1830–1859) would not allow stamps to be stamped by the post office.

◆ George V (reigned 1910–1936) kept hundreds of clocks in his house at Sandringham – all of them exactly 30 minutes fast.

If you wish to extend the activity, you could use these royal facts.

◆ Catherine The Great of Russia (reigned 1762–1796) imprisoned her hairdresser in an iron cage for three years.

◆ Queen Juana of Spain (reigned 1504–1506) always took her dead husband with her in a coffin when she travelled.

◆ Ludwig II of Bavaria (reigned 1864–1886) used to shoot a peasant each morning from his bedroom window – unknown to him the gun was loaded with blank bullets and the peasant pretended to die.

◆ As a boy, King Edward VI (reigned 1547–1553) had a friend who was smacked whenever the king was naughty.

◆ Philippe, Duke of Orleans (1640–1701) had to wear dresses and play with dolls until he was 12 years old.

◆ Shih Huang Ti (Qin dynasty) (reigned 221–210BC) slept in a different palace each night.

◆ King Mithridates VI of Pontus in Asia Minor took small doses of poison each day.

◆ General Jan Zizka of Bohemia (c. 1358–1424) ordered the skin to be removed from his body after his death and used in making a drum.

Extracts from *The Guinness Book of Oddities* © 1995 Geoff Tibballs and Guinness Publishing Ltd.

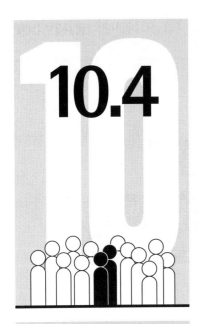

10.4 Rules and lines

Before class
Make one copy of the **Game sheet** (p.85) for each group of two or three learners.

In class
1 This game is based on learners' knowledge of the rules of well-known sports that are played around the world.

2 Divide the class into groups of two or three learners. Give each group a **Game sheet** and ask members of the class which sport each illustration relates to. The sports illustrated are as follows: 1–tennis; 2–basketball; 3–football; 4–American football; 5–darts.

Point out the line markings in each illustration. Tell learners that this activity is related to the line markings and the rules relating to those markings.

Some of the lines are lettered. Explain to learners that they should write down rules pertaining to these lines.

Each group has to write one rule for four to six of the lettered lines. These rules can relate to any lettered line in any illustration. For example:

The game has to restart on this line.	P
You mustn't pass the ball back across this line.	L
You have to cross this line to score.	A
You have to finish the game within these lines.	Y

Learners should write rules with letters which, when read out in order, spell a word. For example, P + L + A + Y above: PLAY.

Go around the class helping groups as they write their rules. When each group has written the rules, you are ready to begin the game.

3 The aim of the game is to be the first group to work out the word that the rules (lettered) spell out.

4 Ask one group to start reading their rules, pausing after each one. Learners should read them out in the sequence that spells the word. While they do this, members of all the other groups should look at the illustrations and try and work out which line a rule relates to. As soon as the players in a group think that they might know the word the lines spell, they should shout it out. The first group to get the correct answer scores a point.

5 The group that has scored the most points at the end of the game wins.

Level
intermediate

Class size
groups of two or three

Language focus
use of *must*, *have to*, *don't have to*, *mustn't*, *can*, *can't*, to talk about rules

Pronunciation
weak forms: *must* /məs/ *mustn't* /mʌsnt/ *can* /kən/ *have to* /həv tə/

Preparation time
5 minutes

Game time
25 minutes

Game sheet

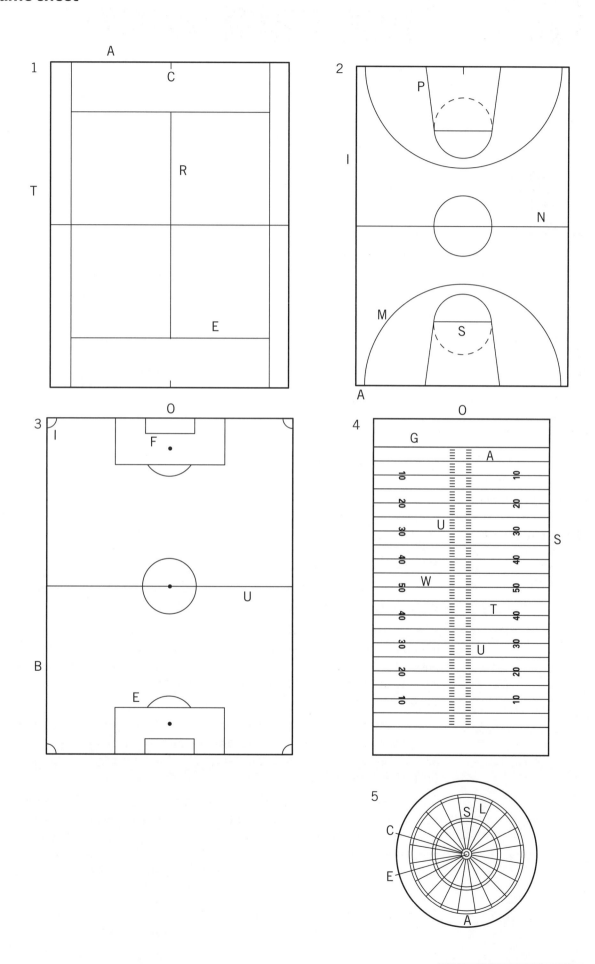

11.1 Last card wins

Level
pre-intermediate – intermediate

Class size
groups of four

Language focus
common prepositional phrases: *on foot, in cash, at night*

Pronunciation
weak forms: *at* /ət/ *for* /fə/

Preparation time
10 minutes

Game time
25 minutes

Before class
Make one copy of the **Question sheet** (p.87) for each pair of learners.
Give each pair of learners 16 blank cards and two wild cards – cards with jokers – (also p.87).

In class
1 In this card game, the last player to lay a card wins each round.

2 Divide the class into pairs. Elicit from learners a few words from the following categories: means of transport, times of the day, means of payment. Do not worry about or give correct prepositional forms at this stage.

Now give each pair 16 blank cards and two wild cards. Give each pair a question sheet and explain to learners that what they have to do is to think of short prepositional phrases that could answer these questions. For example:

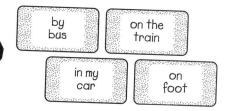

Learners need to think of two or three answers to each question and write each separate answer on one of the blank cards. They must, however, write on all their blank cards. Encourage learners where possible to think of more unusual answers as this will be to their advantage.

3 Seat one pair opposite another pair against whom they will be playing. Pair A starts by asking Pair B the first question: *How did you get here?*

Pair B now has to put down an appropriate prepositional phrase. Pair B then asks the same question to Pair A. Pair A has to put down another appropriate prepositional phrase. This continues until one pair runs out of appropriate cards to put down. The last pair to put down a prepositional phrase wins all the cards.

Pair A cannot put down the same phrase as Pair B and vice versa. If at any time, one pair thinks the other pair has put down an inappropriate or incorrect phrase they should challenge and if it is agreed to be wrong (you may act as judge) they win the card.

A wild card can be played at any time. Students simply provide an oral answer to the question as they play the card. Thus a pair can win a round even if they have run out of cards with appropriate prepositional phrases on. The round ends once a wild card has been played. If it is agreed that the wild card answer is correct, the pair playing the card wins all the cards; if it is decided that it is not correct, the other pair wins the cards.

4 Pairs take it in turns to start a round with a new question. The pair with the most cards at the end of the game, i.e. when all the questions have been asked, wins.

Question sheet

How did you get here? **(means of transport)**	Where did you leave your bag? **(some form of public transport)**
When did she call you? **(time of day [not clock time])**	How did you pay? **(means of payment)**
Where did you put the key? **(somewhere in the living room)**	When do people get presents? **(what special days)**

11.2 Opposite moves

Before class

Make one set of the **Sentence cards** and one set of the **Opposite cards** (p.89) for each group of three learners (six learners if the game is played in pairs).

On the back of the **Sentence cards** write the verb + preposition opposite the highlighted phrase in the sentence (key below).

In class

1 This game is a simple card game based on matching opposites.

2 Divide the class into groups of three (six if the game is to be played in pairs).

3 Give each group one set of both the **Sentence cards** and **Opposite cards** and ask one of the three players to deal an equal number of **Opposite cards** face-down to each player. Tell players to pick up their cards and conceal them from other players. When this has been done, place a set of the **Sentence cards** in the middle of each group, with the sentence on the first card showing. All the sentence cards should be in a pack sentence-side up, i.e. so the opposite phrase is hidden.

4 Ask one player in the group to write the name of each player on a piece of paper.

Nominate one player to start. He/she picks up the **Sentence card** and places it in the middle of the group. This player then has the first option to lay down an **Opposite card** from his/her hand, i.e. a card which he/she believes corresponds to the 'opposite' phrase written on the back of the **Sentence card**. The two other players can then also lay down an **Opposite card** if they wish. The **Sentence card** is then turned over.

The person who has put down the correct **Opposite card** is the winner of the round. He/she keeps the **Sentence card**. If no-one is correct, the sentence is simply put at the bottom of the pack.

If a player puts down a card which is incorrect, he/she has an 'X' written against his/her name on the piece of paper.

Players take back their **Opposite cards** each time.

The game continues with a different player starting each round.

5 The game ends when either all the **Sentence cards** have been used or when one player has three Xs against his or her name. The winner of the game is the player with the most Sentence cards at the end.

Key:

He **left** Spain on Friday. (arrived in)
We **drove through** Luxembourg. (stopped in)
The cat **climbed up** the tree. (got down from)
The door was locked but we still **got in**. (got out)
We **boarded** the plane quickly. (got off)
The train **passed through** two stations. (stopped at)
He **arrived from** Italy yesterday. (went to)
She opened the car door and **got out**. (got in)
The cars **went onto** the ferry smoothly. (came off)
She **went in** just before the end. (came out)

The train **left** the station on time. (arrived at)
She **got off** the bus. (got on)
The train **arrived at** platform six. (left from)
She **got in** her car and left. (got out of)
They **walked away from** us. (came towards)
The rabbit **came out of** its hole. (went into)
He got there after we **arrived**. (departed)
They **left** home yesterday. (went back)
We **came out of** the main entrance. (went in through)
Sheila **went to** the fridge. (moved away from)

Level
upper-intermediate

Class size
groups of three (or six)

Language focus
prepositions complementing verbs of movement

Pronunciation
weak forms: at /ət/ to /tə/ into /ɪntə/ of /əv/

Preparation time
10 minutes

Game time
25 minutes

Sentence cards

He *left* Spain on Friday.	The train *left* the station on time.	We *drove through* Luxembourg.	She *got off* the bus.
The cat *climbed up* the tree.	The train *arrived at* platform six.	The door was locked but we still *got in*.	She *got in* her car and left.
We *boarded* the plane quickly.	They *walked away from* us.	The train *passed through* two stations.	The rabbit *came out of* its hole.
He *arrived from* Italy yesterday.	He got there after we *arrived*.	She opened the car door and *got out*.	They *left* home yesterday.
The cars *went onto* the ferry smoothly.	We *came out of* the main entrance.	She *went in* just before the end.	Sheila *went to* the fridge.

Opposite cards

arrived in	arrived at	stopped in	got on
got down from	left from	got out	got out of
got off	came towards	stopped at	went into
went to	departed	got in	went back
came off	went in through	came out	moved away from

11.3

Time pieces

Level
pre-intermediate –
intermediate

Class size
groups of three (or six)

Language focus
Use of *in, at, on* in
prepositional time phrases

Pronunciation
weak form: *at /ət/*
primary stress in
noun phrases:
Monday morning etc

Preparation time
5 minutes

Game time
25 minutes

Before class

Make one copy of the three **Preposition circles** and one copy of the **Game board** (p.91) for each group of three learners (six learners if played in pairs). You will also need one dice for every three learners and one counter for each player (preferably different colours).

In class

1 This is a board game where players race against each other to get all the pieces they need.

2 Divide the class into threes (or groups of six, composed of three pairs). Give each group a **Game board** and a dice.

Seat the three learners round the board and give each learner (or pair) one of the **Preposition circles** (either *in, at* or *on*) and a counter.

3 The aim of the game is to be the first player to have a complete circle.

How to play:

4 Nominate one player to start.

Players take it in turns to roll the dice and move to a different square around the **Game board** according to the number indicated on the dice. Players can move in any direction around the board with any throw of the dice.

The aim of the game is to land on squares where the time phrase can be complemented by the preposition in the circle. Thus a player with the *at* circle would try to land on squares such as: FOUR O'CLOCK, CHRISTMAS etc.

When a player lands on such a square, he/she should say that he/she wishes to write the word in one of the six segments of his/her circle, e.g.

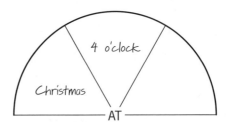

If, however, a player wishes to write a word in his/her circle that neither of the other players thinks fits, that player then misses a throw next time. The teacher can act as referee where a difference of opinion remains. If he/she lands on a square he/she cannot use, the turn simply moves on to the next player.

The winner is the first player to complete his/her circle with time phrases.

Preposition circles

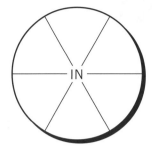 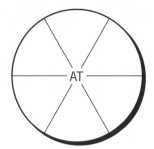 

Game board

MY BIRTHDAY		CHRISTMAS DAY	THE SIXTIES		FOUR O'CLOCK	JUNE
			5th JUNE			THE TWENTIETH CENTURY
LUNCHTIME			1945			FRIDAY
THE WEEKEND			TUESDAYS	THE EARLY HOURS	SPRING	
THE EVENING						MONDAY MORNING
			EASTER			CHRISTMAS
THURSDAY EVENING	THE MOMENT	MIDNIGHT		WEEKDAYS	NIGHT	START

11.4

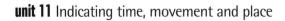

Preposition chequers

Level
pre-intermediate –
intermediate

Class size
groups of three (or six)

Language focus
contrast between *in*, *at*
and *on* to indicate place

Pronunciation
weak forms: *a* /ə/ *an* /ən/

Preparation time
15 minutes

Game time
25 minutes

Before class
Make one copy of the **Chequers board**, **Counters** and **Playing cards** (pp.93–4)
for every three or six learners depending on the size of the class.

In class
1 This game is based on the traditional board game of Chinese chequers where
players try to get across the board as quickly as possible.

2 Arrange the class so that the three players (six if played in pairs) are sitting
around the game board in front of one of the 'start' positions and facing one of
the 'home' positions on the board.

Give each player (or pair) one set of the counters. The three sets of counters are
shaded differently so a player can always identify his/her counters on the board.

Ask each player to place his/her counters on their 'start' position of the board
and you should then place a set of playing cards 'face-down' next to the game
board when players are ready to start.

3 The aim of the game is to be the first player (or pair) to get all his/her
counters to his/her home position on the other side.

How to play:

4 Nominate one player to pick up a card. Tell the player to show the card to
the player on his/her left but to conceal the preposition on the card with
his/her thumb. The player to the left then has to say which preposition of
place (*in/at/on*) completes the phrase.

If the player is correct: He/she can move the appropriate counter (*in/at/on*
counter) to an adjoining space on the board. The direction does not matter
but the aim is to get the counters across the board. However, he/she cannot
move a counter onto a space that is already occupied and does not have to
move if he/she prefers. The card is placed at the bottom of the pile of cards.

If the player is wrong: The card is simply placed at the bottom of the pile
without the correct answer being revealed.

The player who was asked in the previous turn then picks up a card and
continues the game with the player on his/her left, and so on.

5 The winner of the game is the first player/pair to get all their counters home.

Chequers board

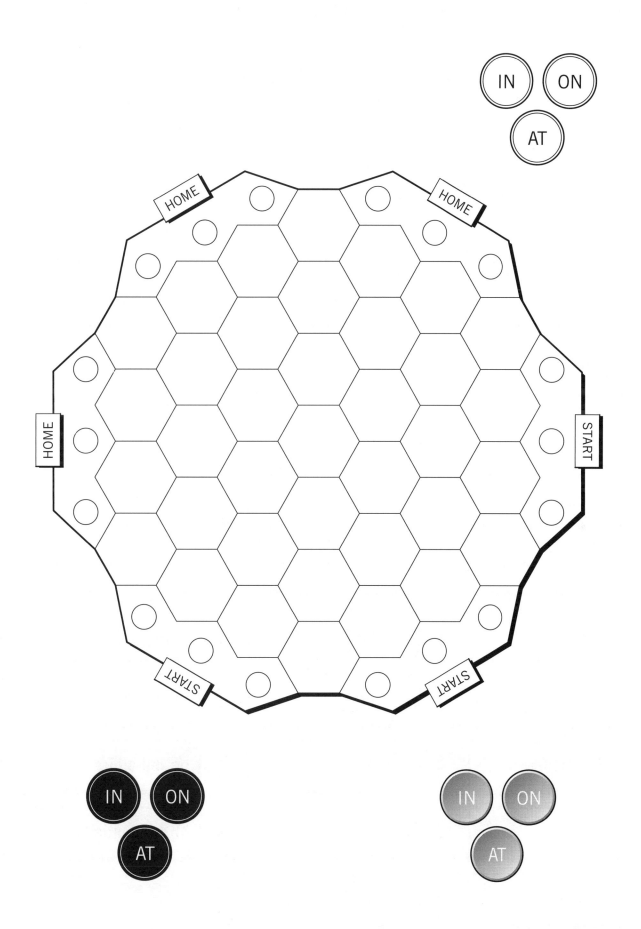

11.4 Preposition chequers

in bed	in Asia	in prison
on TV	at Peter's	on earth
at home	at a party	on a map
in hospital	at the roadside	in the country
in paradise	on an island	on the radio
at university	on the coast	at the seaside
at the bus-stop	at the traffic lights	in an armchair
in the newspaper	in the corridor	in the bathroom
on a mountain	on the sofa	on the River Thames
on a motorway	at the North Pole	at the end of the road
at the back of the room	in a lift	in the world
in the middle	in the mirror	on the stairs
on a course	on a shelf	at the dentist's
at customs	at the checkout	

94 From **The Grammar Activity Book** by Bob Obee © Cambridge University Press 1999 **PHOTOCOPIABLE**

Signs of the passive

12.1

Before class

Cut out the **Passive pictures** (p.97) and stick them on the walls/notice-boards/blackboard etc. around the classroom so that when playing the game learners will be able to get to them easily. Enlarge them if you think it is necessary.

Make one copy of the **Participle sign cards** (p.96) for each group of four to five learners. Cut these out making one set for each group and making sure that all the cards are in the same order in each set. Take some re-usable adhesive to class so that the **Participle sign cards** can be stuck to the pictures.

In class

1 This is a game where players race to match signs to the contexts in which they are found.

2 Divide the learners into groups of four or five and arrange the class so that each group has a 'home' desk/area separate from the other groups. Near to each group – but not within immediate reach – place one set of the **Participle sign cards** face-down. Remember the cards in each set should be in the same order.

Explain to learners they are going to play a game in which they have to recognise where they would see certain signs. Point out the pictures that are on the walls and explain that in each round of the game, they will have to match one of the **Participle sign cards** to the place where it would normally be found as a sign.

3 The aim of the game is to be the first group to match the sign to its context and explain the 'passive' meaning.

4 To play the game, each group puts a different player forward for each round. Number the players in each team (1, 2, 3 etc.) and call out a different number each round. Start each round by saying '*go*'. The players go to their pile of **Participle sign cards**, pick up the top card and try and put it with the right picture before any of the other players from the other teams (remember: all the sets of cards should be in the same order so that groups are racing to find the picture for the same word in each round). Group members can help them find the right picture by shouting out.

The group that gets to the picture first gets one point and has the chance to win another point, if they can produce correctly a full (passive) sentence that explains the meaning of the sign. All members of the group can consult. For example,

Toilet on plane: **OCCUPIED**   *The/This toilet is occupied* (correct)
                                 but not: *The toilet be/was occupied* etc. ...

If the answer given by the first group is incorrect, open the question to all the other groups and the first person to shout out a correct sentence wins one point for their group. Keep a running score. Players who did not succeed in a round should give their cards to the teacher.

For some signs more than one correct interpretation is possible. For example, **DELAYED**: your flight plan has been/will be delayed, but not: ... was delayed.

5 The group that has the most points after all the cards have been used wins.

Level
intermediate

Class size
groups of four or five

Language focus
the use of the passive in signs; use of the passive with different tenses.

Pronunciation
weak forms: *has* /həz/
been /bɪn/

Preparation time
10 minutes

Game time
25 minutes

12.1 Signs of the passive

CHECKED	OCCUPIED	DELAYED
SOLD OUT	INSTALLED	POSTPONED
RESERVED	REDUCED	SOLD
LOST AND FOUND	WANTED	TO BE CONTINUED
	PAID	

From **The Grammar Activity Book** by Bob Obee © Cambridge University Press 1999 **PHOTOCOPIABLE**

Passive pictures

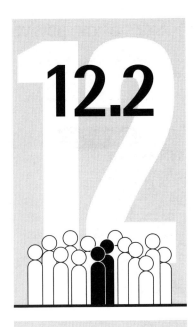

12.2 Whose house?

Before class

Make a copy of each of the '**Whose house?**' cards (p.99). You'll need a different '**Whose house?**' card for each group of two or three learners.

Popular characters from children's fiction have been chosen for this game. If you think some of the characters are not appropriate for your class, change some of the cards for characters they know.

In class

1 This is a deduction game where in each round an extra clue is given about the identity of a well-known fictional character.

2 Give each group of two or three learners a different '**Whose house?**' card. Tell them not to reveal to the other groups whose house they have got.

Point out to learners that on their cards there are four sentences (using a passive form) that give clues as to whose house it is. Ask learners to complete the cards with three more 'passive' clues about whose house it is. Encourage them to think of the person's tastes, what he/she might do at home, objects he/she might have around etc. For example:

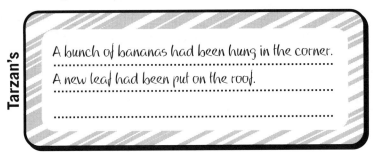

Tarzan's
A bunch of bananas had been hung in the corner.
A new leaf had been put on the roof.

3 As groups do this, go around helping each group with vocabulary, and elicit correct passive forms where learners are having problems.

To start the game, ask one group to read out their first clue. Give the other groups a few seconds to confer/guess whose house it is. If no-one makes a guess, ask the group to read the next clue and so on.

4 Each group has one guess at whose house it is. If the group guesses incorrectly, it is eliminated from this round and cannot make any further guesses after any of the other clues. Learners, therefore, need to be quite cautious.

5 The group that guesses correctly scores as follows:

after 1 clue: 7 points   5 clues: 3 points
     2 clues: 6 points   6 clues: 2 points
     3 clues: 5 points   7 clues: 1 point
     4 clues: 4 points

Write this scoring system on the board. When one group has guessed correctly move onto a new house with a new set of clues. Keep a running score so that there is a winning group at the end.

Sidebar

Level
upper-intermediate

Class size
groups of two or three

Language focus
past forms of the passive in narrative description

Pronunciation
weak forms: *had* /həd/ *been* /bɪn/ *was* /wəz/

Preparation time
10 minutes

Game time
30 minutes

12.2 Whose house?

'Whose house?' cards

Dracula's

A large wooden box had just been polished in the lounge.
In the bathroom a set of false teeth had been put in a glass to soak.
A black cloak had been hung out to dry in the garden.
An eyebrow pencil had been left by the mirror.

....
....
....

Three Bears'

The front door had been left open.
Some food had been left to cool in the kitchen.
The table had been set up for three people.
A chair had been broken.

....
....
....

Tom and Jerry's

The fridge had been recently raided.
The dog had been put in his kennel for the night.
A small hole had been made in the wall.
A lot of damage had been done in the lounge.

....
....
....

Star Trek crew's

An announcement had just been made by the captain.
A new course had been set.
Someone had just been made to disappear.
A few pills were eaten for lunch.

....
....
....

Batman's

The door was answered by a butler.
A special extension had been built in the basement.
A few pictures had been hung upside down.
A special lock had been put on the wardrobe.

....
....
....

Sherlock Holmes'

A cap had been hung up in the hall.
Some pipe tobacco had been put by the fireplace.
A violin could be heard in the next room.
A magnifying glass had been removed from its case.

....
....
....

From **The Grammar Activity Book** by Bob Obee © Cambridge University Press 1999 **PHOTOCOPIABLE**   99

12.3

12

unit 12 Using the passive

A causative day out

Before class

Make one copy of the **Causative town plan** (p.101) for each group of two or three learners and one individual copy for each member of the class. Make one copy (enlarged) for yourself to demonstrate the activity to the class.

In class

1 This is a game where learners have to trace a route dictated by another learner. The route should eventually change into a familiar outline.

2 Explain to learners that you want them to draw a route on a town plan. Tell them the route represents the route they took while visiting the shops in town. Put learners into groups of two or three. Give each group one copy of the town plan.

Ask learners to draw a route linking all the shops/institutions they visited. Explain, however, that this route must be a recognisable shape. For example, a number, a letter, a shape, a simple object etc.

Explain that they will then have to describe their route to the other groups by saying what they had done in each of the shops/institutions they visited: a service performed, not something they bought. They will not be allowed to mention the name of the shop/place, but they can say that they went via this road or that road. For example:

First of all I had my watch mended, then I went via North Street to have my hair done ... .

Give learners time to plan their routes, draw their shape on the plan and discuss what service they had done in each shop. Help groups individually with vocabulary if necessary.

3 The aim of the game is to guess as quickly as possible the shape another group has drawn when they describe their route.

4 Now give out the individual copies of the **Causative town plan** to each learner. Tell learners to mark the routes they hear lightly in pencil so that they can rub out their markings each time.

Ask one group to describe their shopping route to the rest of the class, for example:

I started off from home on the corner of North Lane and Mill Street. I went to have my computer upgraded. I then crossed North Street and had my legs waxed before going via Spring Way to have my stitches taken out. I then went via London Road to have my photos developed before going home.

While listening, members of other groups should try and sketch the route. The first learner to shout out what the recognisable shape is, wins a point for his/her team. (In the example it is the letter 'A'.)

If no-one gets the route the first time, ask a different member of the group to describe the route again.

5 The winners of the game are the group with the most points after all the routes have been described.

Level
upper-intermediate

Class size
groups of two or three

Language focus
talking about *having/getting things done* and the places where you would typically have them done

Pronunciation
linking: *had͜ our my͜ eyes*

Preparation time
5 minutes

Game time
25 minutes

Causative town plan

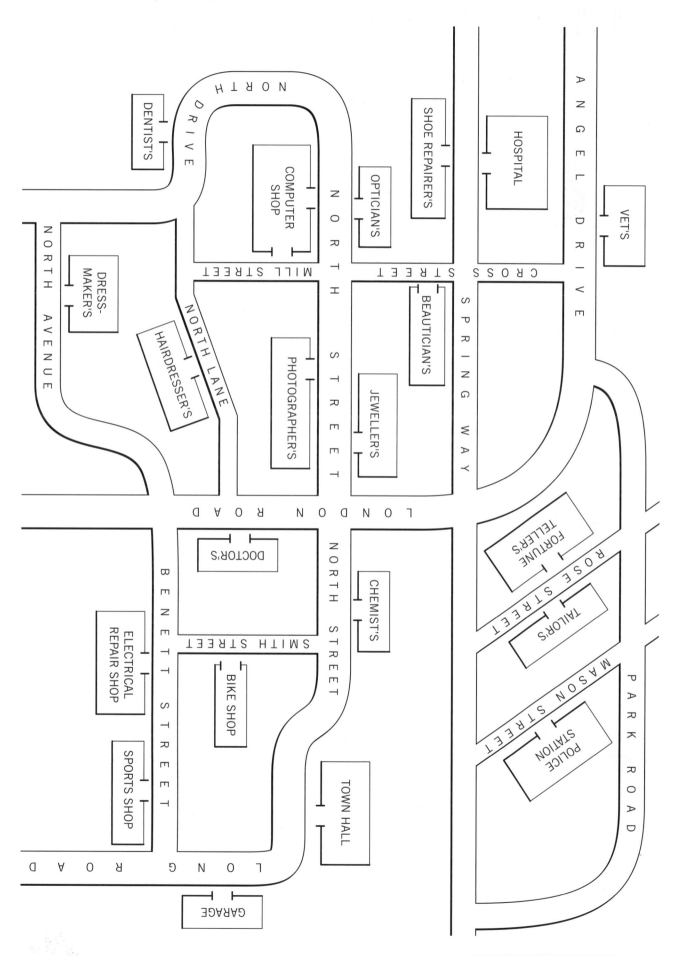

unit 12 Using the passive

12.4 Fairytale jigsaw races

Before class

Make one copy of one **Fairytale jigsaw sheet** (p.103) for each group of two or three learners. If you think that your learners are unlikely to be familiar with some of the stories, erase some of the names of the stories and replace them with ones that you feel are more appropriate.

Bring to class several pairs of scissors so that groups can cut out their jigsaws.

In class

1 This is a game where learners make jigsaws for other groups to put together based on events in well-known fairytales (stories).

2 Give each group of two or three learners one copy of one jigsaw sheet. Get learners to look at the example sentences on their jigsaw sheet and tell them that they have to complete all the empty pieces in a similar way, i.e. with two passive sentences that describe actions or events from the story but do not name any of the characters.

Two important things to make clear to learners are:
a Events described in the left-hand pieces of the jigsaw must come earlier in the story (see Cinderella) than events described in the right-hand pieces of the jigsaw.

b When learners are writing the clues in the right-hand side of the puzzle, they should write them upside-down, as in the example (next to Pinnochio).

Where the jigsaw peice is marked 'choose your own', learners can select their own story.

While learners are completing their jigsaws, go around the class helping them with any vocabulary and grammar problems.

When learners have completed their jigsaws, ask them to cut out the pieces, shuffle the 21 pieces and put them in a pile next to the central jigsaw piece.

3 The aim of the game is to complete another group's jigsaw correctly before they complete the jigsaw your group gave to them.

4 Ask learners to swap their jigsaw for that of another group. When you say 'go', the groups race against each other to see who can complete the jigsaw correctly the quickest.

5 After one group has played against another, they can take their jigsaw back and play against a further group. Alternatively, they can keep the jigsaw they were given, and swap this in the next match.

Level
intermediate –
upper-intermediate

Class size
groups of two or three

Language focus
use of simple past
passive for narrative events

Pronunciation
weak forms: *was* /wəz/
were /wər/

Preparation time
5 minutes

Game time
30 minutes

Fairytale jigsaw sheet

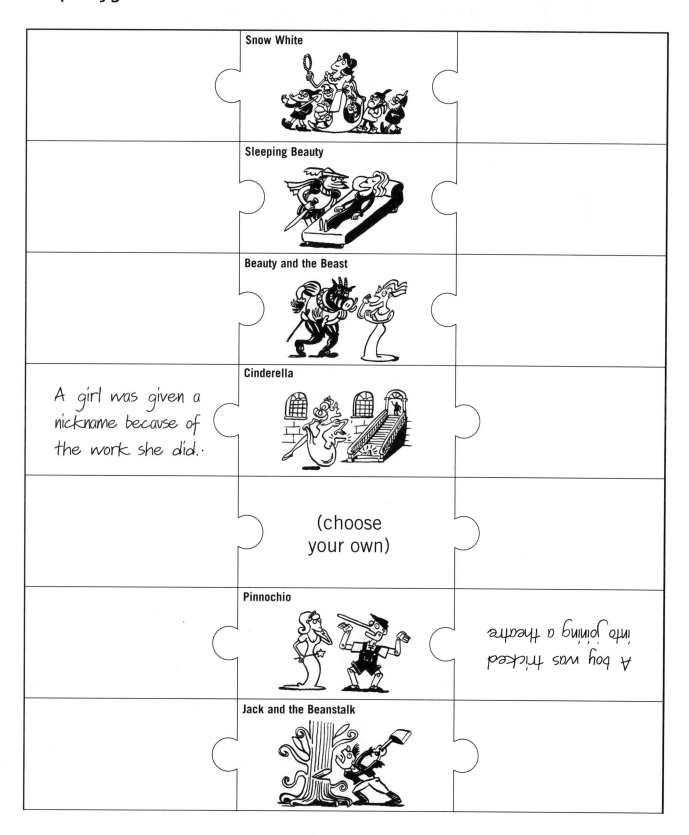

13.1 Answer keys

Level
pre-intermediate –
intermediate

Class size
groups of two or three

Language focus
appropriate answers in
short exchanges

Pronunciation
fall–rise intonation
(seeking response):
Shall I ask? Do you mind?

Preparation time
5 minutes

Game time
25 minutes

Before class
Make one copy of the **Game board** (p.105) and a copy of the **Bunches of keys** (below) for each group of two or three learners. Cut the pictures of the bunches of keys out so that each bunch can be given to students separately.

In class
1 This is a game where learners have to solve a puzzle to reveal a correct sequence of letters. The teacher is the only person that knows the correct sequence.

2 Divide learners into groups of two or three and give each group a **Game board**. Explain to learners that you are going to give them three bunches of keys. Tell learners that they are being held prisoner at the top of a tower. To escape, they have to find the bunch of keys that will open all the doors on each level of the tower. For each level of the tower there is only one bunch of keys that contains appropriate responses to what is written on all the doors they have to pass through.

3 The aim of the game is to be the first to reveal to the teacher the correct sequence of letters.

4 Give the command for the game to start. When a group finds the correct bunch of keys for the level they should write the bunch letter (A, B or C) down and move on to the next level.

5 The first group of students to reveal to you the correct sequence of letters upon escaping the tower [CBABC] wins the game. If a group gives you the wrong answer send them back into the tower to try again.

Bunches of keys

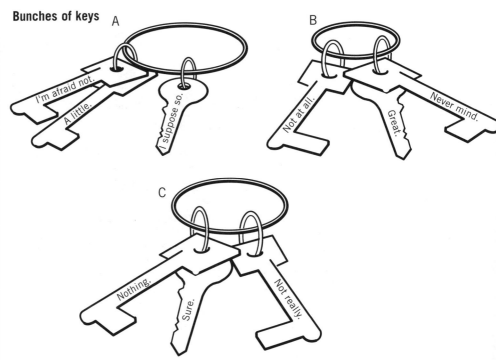

Game board

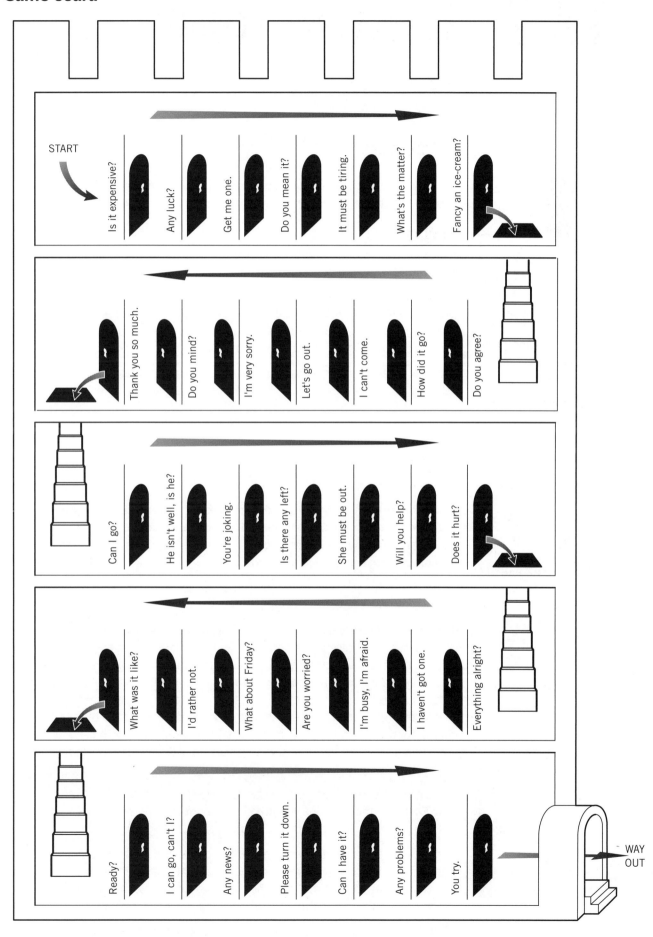

13.2 On the floor debate

Before class

Make one copy of the **Phrase sheet** (p.107) for each group of three members of class. Cut out each word/phrase on the sheets and put everything into an envelope so that each group can be given a complete set of the words/phrases.

In class

1 This is a game where learners engage in a debate with the aim of using all the language in front of them.

2 Before starting the discussion, it is a good idea to do some pre-work with the language on the sheet. You might, for example, ask learners to group the language according to function. You could also ask learners to spot phrases which require them to continue speaking if they use them, e.g. *Look, The way I see it,* ...

Set the context of the debate by explaining to learners that a world-famous celebrity (choose a person or group the whole class knows, or ask the class to choose) is coming to visit their school and local area. In their groups, learners should draw up a morning and afternoon itinerary for the visit. The programme should include about five or six things to do, including some event at the school, e.g.

A.M. Concert: school band   P.M. Visit local farm

Once learners have started discussing and noting down the itinerary, give each group in turn one particularly contentious event to include in their programmes, e.g. go to swimming pool after lunch, take him/her to local barber shop for a haircut, ask him/her to be in school play etc. ...

3 The aim of the game is to be the first group to have used all the language/phrases correctly during the course of the debate.

4 When each group has a rough itinerary for the visit, begin the debate. Learners should arrange the discussion phrases in front of them so that any member of the group can get to them quickly. Tell students that the whole class is now going to discuss their itineraries and that the aim of the game is to be the first team to get rid of all the language in front of them. To do this, they simply have to use the language at functionally appropriate points in the debate and, as they say each phrase, to throw it on the floor. If they use the phrase correctly, it stays on the floor; if not, indicate that they have to pick it up and look for another opportunity to use it. For example:

A: ***Look*** (phrase on floor) *she wants to see something local and traditional.*
B: ***Exactly*** (phrase on floor) *so we should perform a local dance.*
C: ***So what!*** (phrase on floor but told to pick it up again).

To start the debate, just ask one group to outline part of their programme. Any member of this group or any other group can then 'throw in' a phrase or take over the turn at any point. When the debate seems to be drying up, ask another group to start outlining a different part of their itinerary.

5 The first team to have correctly 'thrown in' all the phrases during the debate wins.

Level
intermediate – upper-intermediate

Class size
groups of three

Language focus
commonly used phrases in discussion: *no way, exactly, why's that?* etc

Pronunciation
intonation – rising (continuation): *Look* falling: (closing) *No way*

Preparation time
5 minutes

Game time
30 minutes

Phrase sheet

Rubbish!	The way I see it, ...
That's not the point.	Of course.
You're joking.	No way!
Exactly.	What's that?
I see what you mean.	So what!
Really?	Maybe, but ...
I'm not so sure.	If you ask me, ...
So what you're saying is ...	Look, ...

13.3 Conversation pyramids

Before class

Make one copy of the **Pyramid puzzle** (p.109) for each group of three learners. Cut it out and put the jumbled pieces of each puzzle in separate envelopes.

In class

1 Explain to learners that the game they are going to play involves them putting the pieces of a puzzle together to make a pyramid. Draw this on the board.

2 Tell learners that each triangle represents a short three-part dialogue: question/statement – response – follow-up. For example:

A *How are you?*
B *Not very well.*
C *What's the matter?*

Where a triangle has a blank side, this means that this triangle shares a common side with another triangle, e.g.

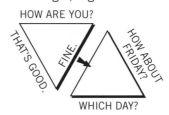

Thus some questions/responses etc. are part of more than one dialogue. Learners complete the pyramid by joining the triangles up in this way.

3 The aim is to be the first group to complete the pyramid by working out how the dialogue sequences fit together.

4 Put the students into groups of two or three and give each group a jumbled puzzle. Ask groups to discuss how the dialogues fit together and work to solve the puzzle.

5 The winners of the game are the first group to build the pyramid successfully.

KEY:

Level
pre-intermediate – intermediate

Clas size
groups of three

Language focus
short response and follow-ups in conversation: *oh go on, never mind*

Pronunciation
intonation, fall–rise: *Are you coming?* rise–fall: *never mind*

Preparation time
10 minutes

Game time
15–20 minutes

Pyramid puzzle

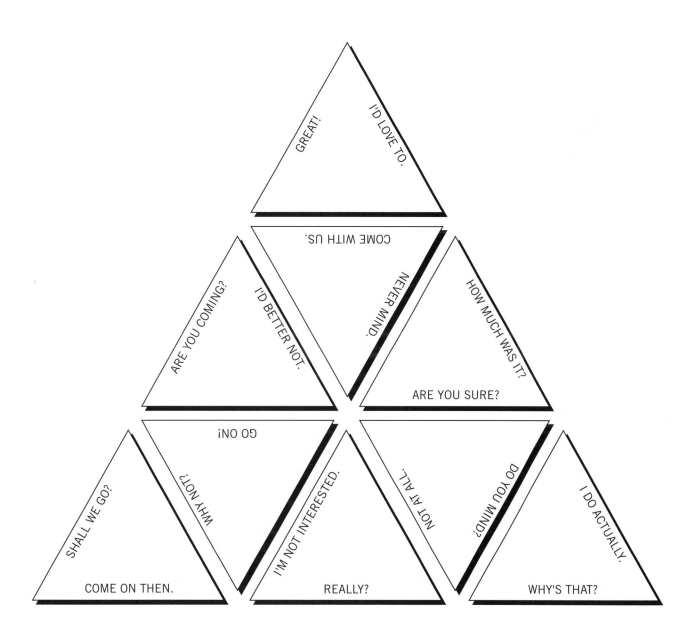

13.4 Answer hopping

Level
elementary –
pre-intermediate

Class size
whole class

Language focus
so/neither responses,
question tags

Pronunciation
falling intonation:
so do I, me too
rise/rise–fall: *She's good,
isn't she?*

Preparation time
15 minutes

Game time
25 minutes

Before class
Write all the words from the **Game grid** (p.111) you choose to use on large
pieces of card. The words on the cards should be clearly visible when stuck to
the floor. Also make three normal size copies of the **Game grid** to stick on the
board. You may also wish to take a whistle to class.

In class
1 This is a game that involves learners helping team members to move from
one side of the room to the other.

2 Divide the class into three teams
(four to seven members). Arrange
the large cut-out pieces on the floor
in the middle of the room (see
pattern on the right).

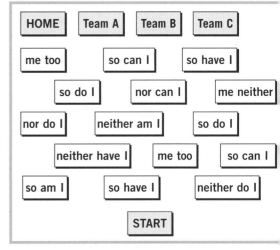

3 Divide the black/whiteboard into
three columns so that each team
has an area to write on. Next to
each column stick a copy of the grid
for learners to refer to during the
game. Ask two learners from each
team to go to their team area at the
black/white board and all other
players to go to the 'start' position
on the other side of the grid.

The 'writers' at the black/whiteboard have to get a player from their team
across the grid on the floor as quickly as possible. They do this by writing on
the black/whiteboard a statement that will allow him/her to move forward on
the grid. For example, if a team writes: *'I don't have any money'* then a player
can move onto the floor by shouting back: *'Neither do I'*. From here, the player
can move to either **'me too'** or **'so can I'** (i.e. one of the two squares
immediately in front). Thus, his/her team members at the black/whiteboard
have to come up with a statement that will allow him/her to do so.

Writers at the black/whiteboard plot the position of players in their team on
their copy of the grid. However, a player can only move to an unoccupied
square. After each successful move, tell writers to rub their statements from
the black/whiteboard.

4 If you spot a team trying to move forward incorrectly, i.e. incorrect statement
(wrong statement–answer match) stop the player (blow the whistle) where
he/she is on the grid. This player can only move forward again when one of the
opposition players currently on the 'floor' gets across. If all three players are
stuck, just give the order for everyone to continue.

When a player successfully gets 'home' he/she replaces one of the writers at the
black/whiteboard, who then joins the rest of his/her team waiting to get home.

5 The winner of the game is the first team to get all members across.

Game grid

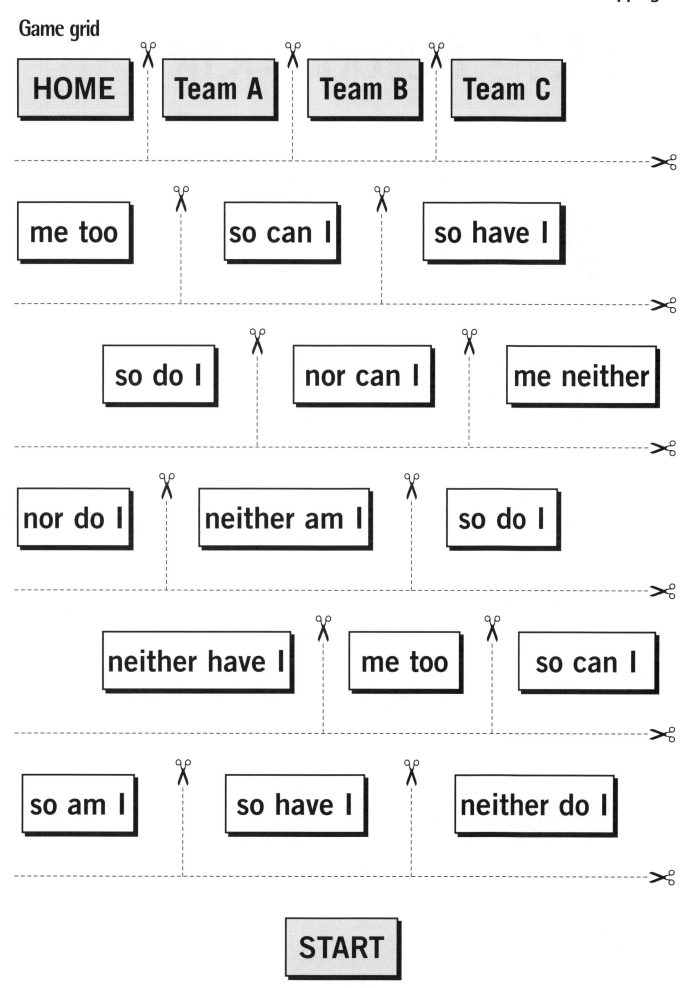

14.1 Beyond belief

Level
intermediate

Class size
groups of three

Language focus
simple reporting structures with *say* and *tell*

Pronunciation
weak form: *that* /ðət/
linking: *told̮us told̮you*

Preparation time
5 minutes

Game time
25 minutes

Before class
Make a copy of one of the **Amazing stories** (p.113) for each group of three to four learners. You may alternatively choose to use stories with which learners are vaguely familiar (in monolingual classes, stories connected with national history work well).

In class
1 This is a story game where learners have to spot inaccuracies or inconsistencies in other groups' stories.

2 Give each group of three students one of the stories on p.113. Tell them not to show it or discuss it with any of the other groups. Make sure you only give out one copy of each story.

Tell each of the groups that what they have to do is change four of the details in the story. They can only change details that have been highlighted. One of the group members should then prepare to read the amended story to the rest of the class.

3 The aim of the game is to try and spot as many inaccuracies or inconsistencies in other groups' stories as possible.

4 A group will probably need to read the story to the class two or three times. When a group has read its story, each of the other groups should say which four details they think have been changed. For example:

*You said they lived on a **ship**. That wasn't true.*

When each of the other groups has done this, the group that told the story then reports to the class what they had changed:

We told you that they were vegetarians. They weren't. They were cannibals. (etc.)

5 If you want, you can keep scores for the groups, awarding one point for every detail they guess to be untrue.

Amazing stories

Swaney Beane and his cannibal family

During the **fifteenth century** there lived a family of **cannibals** in a **cave** in Galloway, Scotland. They are reported to have murdered and eaten more than 1,000 victims over a **20-year period**. In 1435, one of their intended victims escaped from their camp and was able to bring **an army** of 400 **troops**, led by King James I himself, back to their hide-out. There the king found tens of victims pickled and hanging from **the walls** like a butcher's shop. The whole family were captured and taken to Edinburgh and slowly **tortured** and executed without trial.

Beds of nails

Lying on a bed of nails is an old circus and street entertainer trick that dates back **hundreds of years**. On a BBC **television** show in December 1983 a **man** called John Kassar performed probably the most amazing 'bed of nails' stunt ever seen. He lay down on his **back** on a bed of **unblunted**, six-inch nails. A **wooden** board was placed on his **chest** and 29 **girls** climbed on to it. The total weight pressing down on John's body was 3,638 pounds (1,650 kilos). His body was **marked** but the sharp nails did not penetrate his skin.

Rubber-mouth

Rubber-mouth Colin Stevens, a **man** in his **mid-20s** with a **normal** set of teeth, from Sydney, **Australia**, claims that he has the biggest mouth in the world and to prove it he will stuff in 140 cigarettes at a time. In April 1989 he created five new **world** records by stuffing in his mouth: 140 cigarettes, five **golf balls**, six size two **hard-boiled** eggs, one **tennis ball** and one large orange.

A lot of eggs

The largest pancake ever made was produced in 1984 in Vermont, in **the United States**. A **cement truck** was used to mix the mixtures and a **helicopter** to do the flipping of this **six-metre** diameter monster. The four-inch deep pancake contained over 100 gallons of **milk** and 365 kilogrammes of pancake mix, took over two **hours** to cook and could feed **15,000** people. It was topped with 455 kilogrammes of **butter**, 150 gallons of syrup and one quarter of a ton of blueberries.

Pet luxury

German Shepherd **dog** 'Solar' has the world's most expensive kennel. Features in the eight-foot **square brick-built** bungalow-type kennel include net curtains, **fitted carpets**, a four-foot **double bed** with luxury quilt, doggy ornaments on the **window sill**, **electric strip** lighting and running water. The cost to Solar's owner, Mr. Pidd from Humberside, was £3,000.

Snake sacking

In Bolivar, in the United States, they practise the unusual sport of snake sacking. **Five** rattlesnakes are tipped from a **sack at the feet** of the participant who then, with **ungloved** hands, has to grab the snakes and stuff them, **head first**, back into the **sack** which is held open by a colleague. The holder of the world record is Steve Eckenroad, who in April 1988 set a time of **5.49 seconds**. Being bitten means **disqualification!**

14.2 No more than seven words

Before class
Copy the **Prompt cards** (p.115) so that there is one for each member of the class.

In class
1 This is a game which requires learners to report what others say and becomes a game of memory as it progresses.

2 Divide the class into groups of three or four and give one **Prompt card** to each learner. Ask learners to complete their **Prompt cards** with simple sentences for each prompt, each one no more than seven words. For example:

> **Promise:**
> I'll save you a seat.
> **Ask a question:**
> Have you got any change?
> **Ask permission:**
> Can I leave early?

As learners do this, encourage them to help each other within their groups and go around the groups yourself helping with any problems. When they have completed their **Prompt cards**, you are ready to begin the game.

3 The aim of the game is to report correctly as many things said to you as possible.

4 Give each group a letter (A, B, C etc.) and write these letters on the board so that you can keep score. Nominate one player from group A to read out a prompt and one player from group B to report what is said, requested, asked of him/her etc. For example:

> Team A: *Have you got any change?*
> Team B: *He/she asked me if I had/have any change.*

Only allow the prompt to be read once. If the player from group B gets it right, he/she scores two points for his/her group. If not, the first player to shout out the correct answer from one of the other groups wins one point for his/her team.

Nominate a player from group C to read a prompt to a player from group D etc. Continue like this until all players have had a go at reporting.

Following this, you can increase the difficulty of the game by asking two players from one group to read prompts consecutively and nominating a player from another group to report both of them. Score one point for each correct answer.

5 The winning group is the one with the most points at the end of the game.

Level
intermediate –
upper-intermediate

Class size
groups of three of four

Language focus
sentence patterns after various reporting verbs.

Pronunciation
weak form: *that* /ðət/
linking: *asked_if* /ɑːsktɪf/

Preparation time
5 minutes

Game time
30 minutes

Prompt cards

Ask permission:

Promise:

Ask a question:

State a fact:

Demand something:

Ask the time:

Apologise:

Make a prediction:

Make a suggestion:

Ask a question:

Introduce yourself:

Announce something:

Ask for something:

Inquire about someone's health:

Make a suggestion:

Agree with someone:

Tell someone the time:

Make an excuse:

Ask about a friend:

Disagree with someone:

Ask the price:

Make a promise:

Wish for something:

Make a prediction:

Ask permission:

Ask 'why':

Apologise:

Give advice:

Give an order:

Warn someone:

Make a guess:

Offer someone something:

Threaten someone:

Ask 'where':

Demand something:

Refuse permission:

14.3

14

unit 14 What someone said

Connecting speech

Before class
Make one copy of each set of **Connecting speech cards** (p.117) keeping shaded and light cards in separate piles; and one **Game board** (p.118) for every four learners in the group. Put the shaded cards in an envelope marked 'Players 1 and 2' and the light cards in another envelope marked 'Players 3 and 4'.

In class
1 This is a board game where players compete to make lines of phrases which are connected by the same verb of speech.

2 Give each group of four learners one **Game board**. Divide players into pairs so that one pair is playing against another pair. Give one pair the envelope marked 'Players 1 and 2' and the other pair the envelope marked 'Players 3 and 4'. Tell students not to show the other pair their cards.

3 The aim of the game is to get lines (horizontal/vertical/diagonal) of three squares on the board with phrases that all use the same verb, e.g.

4 To play, ask one learner to pick up the top card from their pile, cover the verb with their thumb and show it to the other pair. The other pair now have to say which verb (*say/tell/speak/talk*) starts the phrase.

If they get the answer wrong, the card is simply put to the bottom of the pile. They are not told the correct answer. If they get it right, they can place it on the **Game board**. They can place the card on any square. However, those squares marked with a particular verb can only have phrases put on them that contain the verb. For example, 'fluent French' may be placed on a square marked 'speak' (but not on a square marked 'talk', 'tell' or 'say').

5 The winners of the game are the group with the most lines of three at the end of the game. Any group that gets a line of four automatically wins the game.

Level
intermediate –
upper-intermediate

Class size
groups of four

Language focus
say, tell, speak, talk:
grammatical and meaning
contrasts

Pronunciation
linking: *say it*
'schwa' sounds: *a /ə/*
about /əbaʊt/

Preparation time
10 minutes

Game time
25 minutes

116

Connecting speech cards (players 1 and 2)

... a joke. *tell*	... me something. *tell*	... me the time. *tell*	... a story. *tell*	... him to go. *tell*
... me the truth. *tell*	... sense. *talk*	... to yourself. *talk*	... seriously to me. *talk*	... yes. *say*
... hello from me. *say*	... nothing about it. *say*	... with an accent. *speak*	... after the tone. *speak*	... your mind. *speak*
... rubbish. *talk*	... 'Please'. *say*	... fluent French. *speak*	... her that. *tell*	

Connecting speech cards (players 3 and 4)

... lies. *tell*	... me about it. *tell*	... the word backwards. *say*	... no to her. *say*	... for yourself. *speak*
... Japanese with them. *speak*	... the secret. *tell*	... me the difference. *tell*	... about it with him. *talk*	... nonsense. *talk*
... sorry. *say*	... goodbye to her. *say*	... us the reason. *tell*	... more clearly. *speak*	... up please. *speak*
... business. *talk*	... non-stop. *talk*	... each other anything. *tell*	... him not to. *tell*	

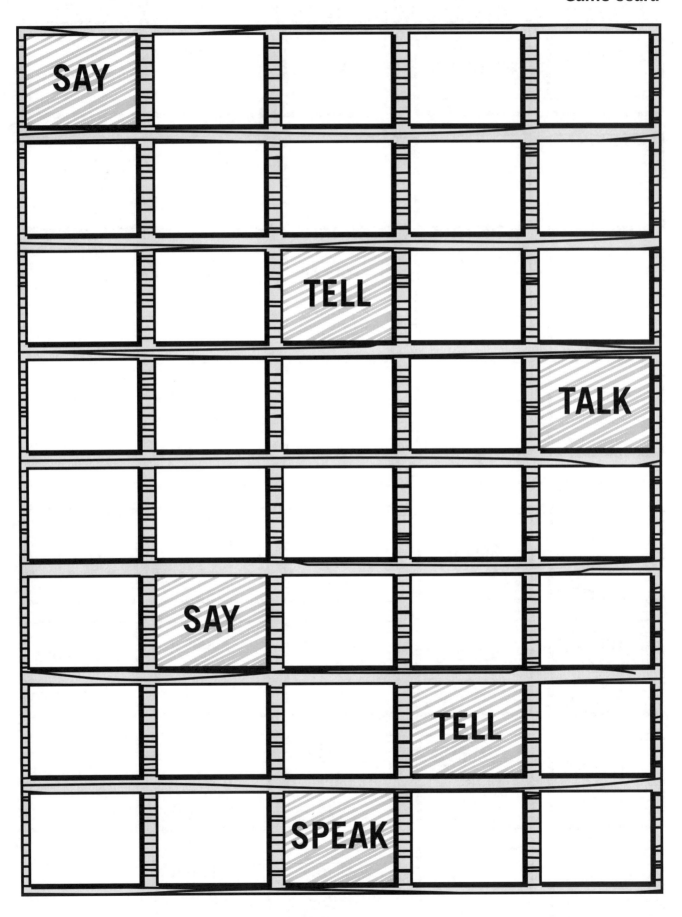

From **The Grammar Activity Book** by Bob Obee © Cambridge University Press 1999 **PHOTOCOPIABLE**

Who asked you ...

14.4

Before class

Before class write on a slip of paper/card a theme for each student in the class. For example:

FAMILY   FREE TIME   GROWING UP   KEEPING FIT

In class

1 This is a memory game where learners have to remember what they were asked during an initial mingling stage.

2 Divide the class into groups of four or five. Give each member a theme card and ask them to write six questions related to the theme. Their questions should not be more than six words in length.

When they have written their questions, ask learners to mingle and ask as many learners as possible from other groups two of the questions. They should vary the questions they ask. Allow about five minutes for this and then ask learners to return to their groups.

3 The aim of the game is to try and remember as many questions that were asked as possible and report these to the group.

4 What learners now have to do in their groups is report to each other what they were asked, in order to work out what the themes behind different learners' questions were.

For example:
- **a:** *Okay, Petra asked me if I had any brothers and sisters.*
- **b:** *And she asked me what job my father does.*
- **c:** *And she asked me something about my grandparents.*
- **a:** *So the theme must be 'family'.*
- **b:** *Alright, François asked if ... etc.*

Allow students about ten minutes to discuss this, so that they have time to work out as many of the themes as possible.

Groups now take it in turns to

a) suggest to the whole class what a class member's theme is:
We think Petra's theme is 'family'.

b) Justify why the group has come to this conclusion:
Because she asked me if I have/had any brothers and sisters.

To win a theme card, a group has to correctly state what the theme was. The teacher should act as judge. If a group does not state correctly what the theme was, or does not report the questions correctly, the card remains to be won in another round.

5 The winner of the game is the group that wins the most theme cards.

Level
intermediate – upper-intermediate

Class size
groups of four or five

Language focus
reported questions

Pronunciation
linking: *who asked asked if*

Preparation time
5 minutes

Game time
30 minutes

15.1 Slide rules

Before class

Make one copy of the **Sentence sheet** and one copy of the **Slide rules** (both p.121) for each group of three learners. Cut the **Slide rules** out so that learners may move them up and down between the parallel lines in the sentences.

From the **Sentence sheet**, select areas of grammar that revise structures taught in class and, where appropriate, think about making up your own sentences and slide rules to practise other structures previously taught in class. Where this is done, you can obviously vary the level of the activity.

In class

1 This is an activity where learners race against each other to fit a group of words into grammatically-correct slots in sentences.

2 Put learners into groups of three. Give each group a **Sentence sheet** and a set of **Slide rules**. Explain to learners that what they need to do is to slot the appropriate slide rule into the sentences and to find the place where it fits.

Example:

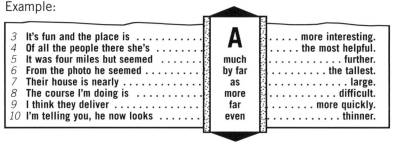

Here is a further example you can use to present the idea to students.

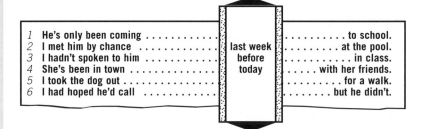

Here, for example, the **Slide rule** fits between 2 and 4. Explain to learners that there is only one place between each group of sentences that the **Slide rule** can fit.

3 When learners have fitted a **Slide rule** into place, they should then write the number of the first sentence of those between which the **Slide rule** fits (e.g. no. 2 for the example above) in the appropriate box at the bottom of the sentence sheet.

4 The winners are the first group to work out where all the Slide rules fit and read out to you the correct sequence of numbers for those slide rules.

Key: A 5	B 6	C 3	D 6

Level
intermediate –
upper-intermediate

Class size
groups of three

Language focus
structures to be revised

Pronunciation
depending on structure

Preparation time
5 minutes

Game time
25 minutes

Sentence sheet

Slide rules

A

1 In my opinion it's definitely . . . . the best.
2 It's not possible to be . . . . quieter.
3 It's fun and the place is . . . . more interesting.
4 Of all the people there she's . . . . the most helpful.
5 It was four miles but seemed . . . . the tallest.
6 From the photo he seemed . . . . the tallest.
7 Their house is nearly . . . . large.
8 The course I'm doing is . . . . difficult.
9 I think they deliver . . . . more quickly.
10 I'm telling you, he now looks . . . . thinner.
11 It was OK but Spain is . . . . better.
12 Her sisters are good but she's . . . . the most talented.

A

much
by far
as
more
far
even

B

1 I didn't think . . . . player was any good.
2 There isn't . . . . news yet.
3 He said that . . . . place has a disco.
4 I don't have . . . . information about it.
5 There must be . . . . room in the new flat.
6 I'm really sure . . . . child meant to do it.
7 We don't have . . . . equipment at school.
8 I'll ask for . . . . glass for you.
9 It's going to last . . . . days this time.
10 Can I have . . . . sugar in mine?
11 We've played . . . . matches this season.
12 I think it takes . . . . time to get there.

B

neither
much
another
several
less
fewer

C

1 He climbed . . . . the tree.
2 I saw her get . . . . the bus.
3 We never got . . . . the station.
4 They've just left . . . . the airport.
5 Are they coming . . . . home?
6 I think he's flying . . . . London.
7 Have they arrived . . . . Paris yet?
8 I'm going to get . . . . at this stop.
9 How can you get . . . . the roof.
10 They've moved . . . . a new flat.
11 We drove straight . . . . the town.
12 I ran all the way . . . . her house.

C

to
for
back
to
in
off

D

1 It has taken . . . . to build.
2 I enjoyed it . . . . two years.
3 I've been living here . . . . now.
4 I have met you . . . . I think.
5 I haven't seen him . . . . at all.
6 He lived there . . . . as a child.
7 I've mentioned it . . . . to her.
8 We haven't played . . . . at all.
9 She spent hours . . . . reading.
10 You've been studying . . . . I suppose.
11 I've had a great time . . . . here.
12 I didn't work . . . . this week.

D

for two years
before
recently
during summer
all week
so far

Numbers **A** _____ **B** _____ **C** _____ **D** _____

15.2 Tense squares

Level
pre-intermediate –
upper-intermediate

Class size
pairs

Language focus
use of different tenses
with time adverbials

Pronunciation
weak forms: *was were has
been have*

Preparation time
5 minutes

Game time
20 minutes

Before class
Below are two different versions of the game – one is for a much lower level class than the other. Select the appropriate version to revise language taught with your class and make one copy for each pair of learners. Note that the game could be adapted to make it even easier or revise other areas of language such as adjective or adverb order.

In class
1 This is a puzzle activity where an image gradually emerges as learners complete the puzzle.

2 Divide the class into pairs and give each pair a copy of the appropriate level **Tense square sheet** (p.123). Explain to the class that they need to find three adverbs that occur in a row (horizontal, vertical or diagonal) on the grid, which can be used to complete the sentences around the outside of the grid.
For example:

He's practising *right now at the moment today.*   [**right now**] [**at the moment**] [**today**]

3 The aim of the game is to shade the correct squares to reveal an image. The pre-intermediate board correctly shaded reveals the image of **steps**. The upper-intermediate board correctly shaded reveals the letter **H**.

4 When learners have found a row of three adverbs for each sentence, they should shade in the squares of these adverbs with a pencil to reveal an image. Please note that there is some overlap in the answers, so learners can use a square that has already been shaded as part of their row of three adverbs.

5 The first group to correctly identify the image wins.

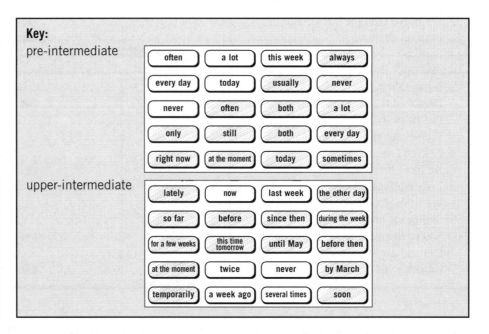

Key:
pre-intermediate

often	a lot	this week	always
every day	today	usually	never
never	often	both	a lot
only	still	both	every day
right now	at the moment	today	sometimes

upper-intermediate

lately	now	last week	the other day
so far	before	since then	during the week
for a few weeks	this time tomorrow	until May	before then
at the moment	twice	never	by March
temporarily	a week ago	several times	soon

Tense square sheet: pre-intermediate

He's practising ___ .   They're ___ having fun.   She works ___ .

often	a lot	this week	always
every day	today	usually	never
never	often	both	a lot
only	still	both	every day
right now	at the moment	today	sometimes

He ___ gets angry.   I don't ___ go there.   They might ___ come.

Tense square sheet: upper-intermediate

I'll be travelling ___ .   I saw her ___ .   I haven't met him ___ .

lately	now	last week	the other day
so far	before	since then	during the week
for a few weeks	this time tomorrow	until May	before then
at the moment	twice	never	by March
temporarily	a week ago	several times	soon

I'm staying here ___ .   I'll have saved enough ___ .   I've been studying hard ___ .

123

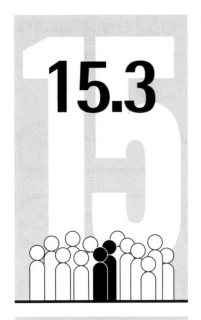

15.3 Throw-out puzzles

Before class

Make one copy of the **Puzzle sheet** (p.125) and cut out the pieces of each puzzle and keep them in separate envelopes. There are sixteen pieces for each puzzle – the twelve pieces on the left and the four 'additional' pieces on the right. As the puzzles are to be used several times even within the one lesson, it might be a good idea to copy them onto cards.

In class

1 This is a jigsaw activity where learners fit together pieces that eventually reveal the outline shape of a country or continent.

2 Divide the class into pairs (or groups of three) and explain to learners that each group will receive a different envelope at the start of each round. Tell learners that inside the envelope there is a jigsaw puzzle. In the envelope there are sixteen pieces. Only twelve pieces, however, are needed to complete each puzzle. Learners, therefore, need to eliminate four pieces. When the puzzle is correctly put together, it reveals the outline shape of a country or continent.

3 The aim of the game is to be the first pair in each round to identify the shape of the country or continent.

4 When you say go, learners empty the pieces onto the desk and try and put the puzzle together by putting lines of three pieces together that fit grammatically. For example:

When learners have put four such lines together to form the whole puzzle – having eliminated the four pieces they don't need – they will have an outline image of a country or continent that they should recognise.

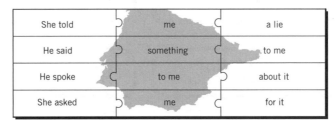

You may want to adapt the country/continent outlines on the puzzles to include ones that might be more readily identifiable for your learners.

The first pair to reveal to you the identity of the country/continent in its puzzle wins the round. Tell learners to write down the name rather than shout it out, as other pairs will have the same puzzle to solve in subsequent rounds.

5 At the end of each round, ask learners to put the pieces of the puzzle back into the envelope and pass the envelopes clockwise round the class so that each pair has a new puzzle to solve. The overall winner of the game is the pair that has won the highest number of rounds.

> **Key:** Images of Spain, Africa, the US, Italy, Greece, Japan.

Level
pre-intermediate

Class size
groups of two or three

Language focus
structures to be revised

Pronunciation
depending on structures

Preparation time
15 minutes

Game time
30 minutes

Puzzle sheet

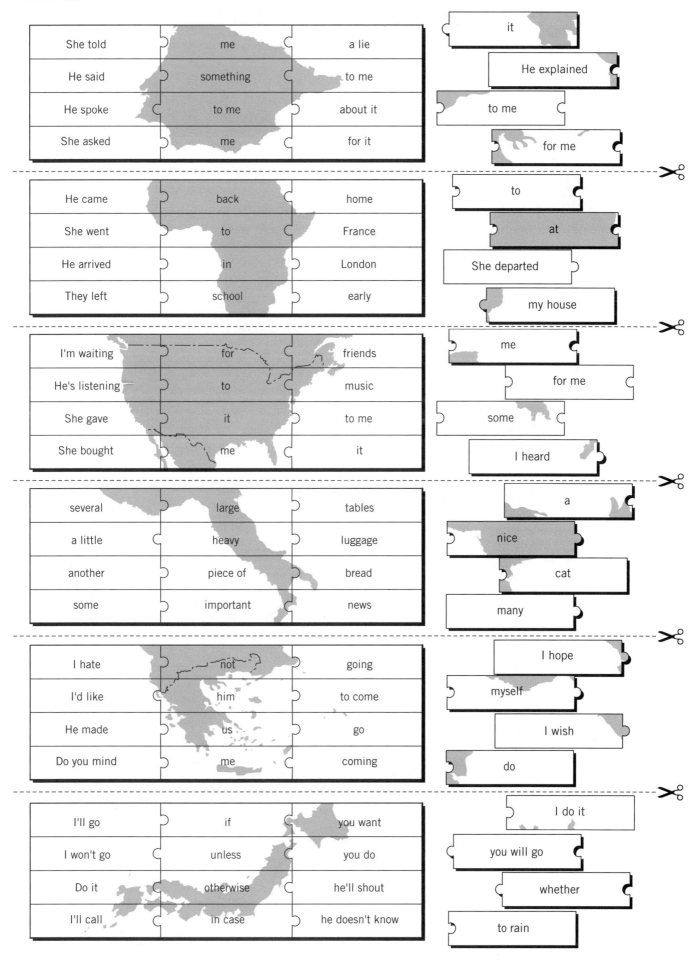

She told	me	a lie
He said	something	to me
He spoke	to me	about it
She asked	me	for it

it
He explained
to me
for me

He came	back	home
She went	to	France
He arrived	in	London
They left	school	early

to
at
She departed
my house

I'm waiting	for	friends
He's listening	to	music
She gave	it	to me
She bought	me	it

me
for me
some
I heard

several	large	tables
a little	heavy	luggage
another	piece of	bread
some	important	news

a
nice
cat
many

I hate	not	going
I'd like	him	to come
He made	us	go
Do you mind	me	coming

I hope
myself
I wish
do

I'll go	if	you want
I won't go	unless	you do
Do it	otherwise	he'll shout
I'll call	in case	he doesn't know

I do it
you will go
whether
to rain

15.4

Level
elementary – intermediate

Class size
whole class

Language focus
various structures
depending on level

Pronunciation
depending on structure

Preparation time
20 minutes

Game time
35 minutes

Sole mates

Before class

There are two sets of **Sole mates** words on the following pages (p.127 and p.128): one for elementary classes and one for intermediate classes. Decide on one of the levels to use, or adapt the task to revise grammar taught recently in your class.

Copy the words onto card (to make them reusable) and with a hole-punch make a hole in one end of each word so you can tie on a piece of string. You will need nine envelopes to keep the words in, marked 'Team A Round 1', 'Team A Round 2' etc. You may also take some re-usable adhesive to class for learners without shoelaces.

In class

1 This is a mingle activity where learners have to find grammatical partners (sole mates) in each round.

2 Divide the class into three teams and ask each team to move to a 'home' desk. Nominate one team to be A, one B and the other C. On each 'home' desk put the appropriate three envelopes, marked 'Round 1', 'Round 2' and 'Round 3'.

You should stand at the front of the class next to an area that is marked LOST SOLES.

At the start of each round ask one learner to empty the contents of the envelope marked for that round onto the desk and ask learners to tie/attach one word to each of their shoes (so it can be seen).

3 The aim of the game is to find a correct grammatical partner or 'sole mate' as quickly as possible in each round, so as to avoid losing your shoes.

4 When you say *go,* members of all teams mingle and approach members of other teams in an effort to find a 'sole mate', i.e. someone who has a word on his/her shoe that is a grammatical partner for one of the words he/she has on his/her shoe.

If one learner feels he/she has found a 'sole mate' and the other learner agrees, they come to you and show you.

If they are correct, they can return to their home area and sit down. If they are not correct, however, each learner has to remove the shoe and place it in the LOST SOLES area.

Learners who have lost a shoe rejoin the mingle. However, they are only allowed to approach others who still have two shoes. If these learners successfully find a partner before the end of the round, they may retrieve their shoe, prior to sitting down. If, however, they lose their second shoe, the shoes remain 'lost soles' until the end of the round. These learners then wait the rest of the round out. The round ends when the last person wearing two shoes has sat down.

5 Scoring: any shoe left in the LOST SOLES area at the end of the round counts as one point against the respective learner's team. The team with the fewest points at the end of the game wins.

Sole mates elementary

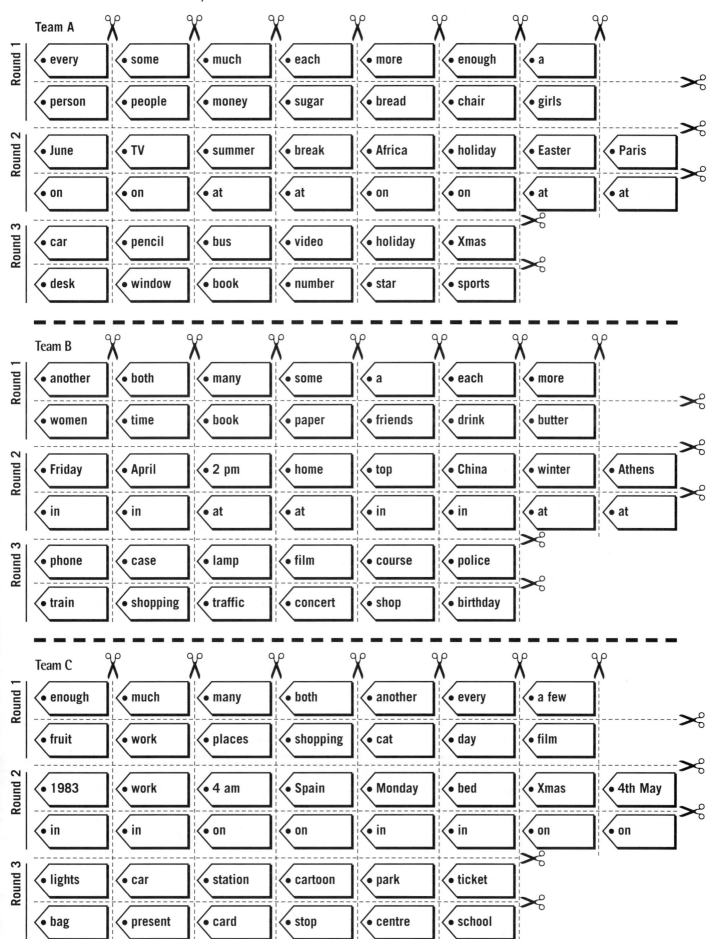

Team A

Round 1	every	some	much	each	more	enough	a	
	person	people	money	sugar	bread	chair	girls	

Round 2	June	TV	summer	break	Africa	holiday	Easter	Paris
	on	on	at	at	on	on	at	at

Round 3	car	pencil	bus	video	holiday	Xmas		
	desk	window	book	number	star	sports		

Team B

Round 1	another	both	many	some	a	each	more	
	women	time	book	paper	friends	drink	butter	

Round 2	Friday	April	2 pm	home	top	China	winter	Athens
	in	in	at	at	in	in	at	at

Round 3	phone	case	lamp	film	course	police		
	train	shopping	traffic	concert	shop	birthday		

Team C

Round 1	enough	much	many	both	another	every	a few	
	fruit	work	places	shopping	cat	day	film	

Round 2	1983	work	4 am	Spain	Monday	bed	Xmas	4th May
	in	in	on	on	in	in	on	on

Round 3	lights	car	station	cartoon	park	ticket		
	bag	present	card	stop	centre	school		

15.4 Sole mates

Sole mates intermediate

Team A

Round 1	kind	fair	active	complete	honest	regular	legal	polite
	ir-	im-	in-	un-	un-	dis-	dis-	in-

Round 2	mood	sugar	care	sleep	success	logic	fashion	smell
	-less	-ful	-ous	-al	-y	-ful	-able	-y

Round 3	several	a few	less	other	many	a	several	some
	news	luck	water	men	shoes	friend	piece	ideas

Team B

Round 1	patient	fit	happy	mature	able	possible	well	rational
	in-	im-	un-	il-	un-	dis-	in-	un-

Round 2	help	music	break	accident	pain	courage	repair	colour
	-less	-ous	-al	-y	-less	-ful	-able	-al

Round 3	much	several	neither	enough	another	less	each	few
	damage	soap	traffic	books	player	shorts	plant	drink

Team C

Round 1	loyal	real	correct	sure	direct	moral	satisfied	literate
	in-	im-	ir-	in-	un-	un-	il-	im-

Round 2	use	risk	danger	dust	like	wonder	health	origin
	-ous	-able	-y	-able	-less	-ful	-ful	-al

Round 3	some	a	each	little	few	enough	neither	much
	luggage	soil	bread	leaves	team	letter	month	eggs

128 From **The Grammar Activity Book** by Bob Obee © Cambridge University Press 1999 **PHOTOCOPIABLE**